Survey of Bedfords[ ]

THE ROMAN PERIOD

by

Angela Simco

Conservation Section, Planning Department
Bedfordshire County Council

BEDFORDSHIRE COUNTY COUNCIL
ROYAL COMMISSION ON HISTORICAL MONUMENTS (ENGLAND)

FOREWORD

The SURVEY OF BEDFORDSHIRE, a joint publication by Bedfordshire County Council and the Royal Commission on Historical Monuments (England), is a study of the county's historic environment, published in sections. Its scope includes archaeology, historic buildings, landscape features and settlement patterns. Sections are devoted to parishes, periods, or selected subjects. Each is complete in itself and contains a descriptive account with a gazetteer.

The SURVEY is intended for all those with an interest in the past of Bedfordshire. It is also a convenient summary of local material for educational use, and a comprehensive guide for the purpose of research.

The SURVEY is largely based upon information in the *Bedfordshire Sites and Monuments Record*, compiled and maintained in the County Planning Department. It draws extensively upon material in the County Record Office.

The first publication arising from the SURVEY was *Brickmaking, a History and Gazetteer* (1979). The series will continue on this occasional basis with volumes being produced as time and resources permit. Other titles are currently in preparation.

The County Council would be grateful to receive any further information on topics covered by the SURVEY. Communications, including requests to consult the Record by appointment, should be addressed to:

Conservation Officer, County Planning Department, County Hall, BEDFORD MK42 9AP.
Telephone: Bedford (STD 0234) 63222.

A.M. Griffin, *County Planning Officer*
Peter Fowler, *Secretary, Royal Commission on Historical Monuments (England)*

April 1984

ACKNOWLEDGEMENTS

In compiling this section of the Survey the help and advice of the following is gratefully acknowledged:

David Baker; Patricia Bell (County Archivist) and the staff of the County Record office, especially Sylvia Woods, James Collett-White and Chris Pickford; Gil Birley (Letchworth Museum), Stephen Coleman, Alan Cox, Mary Cra'ster (Cambridge University Museum of Archaeology and Anthropology), Mike Daniels (Hertfordshire County Council), Stuart Davison (Luton Museum and Art Gallery), Brian Dix, Mike Farley (Buckinghamshire County Museum), Glenn Foard (Northamptonshire County Council), Prof S.S. Frere, Margaret Gelling, Mark Hassall, Martin Henig, Catherine Johns (British Museum), Roy Loveday, Bob Mustoe, Prof A.L.F. Rivet, G.T. Rudd (Longsands School Museum, St Neots), Penny Spencer (Bedford Museum), Alison Taylor (Cambridgeshire County Council), Christopher Taylor (Royal Commission on Historical Monuments), Stanley Warren and John Wood.

Previously unpublished information has kindly been provided by Martin Booth, A.E. Brown, Buckinghamshire Archaeological Society, Eric Compton, Alex Davies, Miss P.B. Dempster, James Dyer, Kevan Fadden and the Ampthill and District Archaeological and Local History Society, Ian Freeman and the Bedford Archaeological Society, Richard Hagen, David Hall, D.C. King, C.L. Matthews and the Manshead Archaeological Society of Dunstable, John Moore, the late I.J. O'Dell, Andrew Pinder, Joan Schneider, Christopher Taylor and Robert White. The bronze mount from Hyde (fig. 42) is illustrated by permission of the Luton Hoo Estate and Mr Edward Bradley. Permission to refer to reports in advance of publication has been given by Pat Aird, Phil Catherall (British Gas), Brian Dix, Stephen Greep, Alison Taylor and Peter J. Woodward.

Thanks are due to John Turner of Bedford Museum (North Bedfordshire Borough Council), Granville T. Rudd of the Longsands School Museum, St Neots, Frank Hackett of Luton Museum and Art Gallery, the Trustees of the British Museum, and Cambridge Univeristy Museum of Archaeology and Anthropology, for their permission to publish items from their collection.

Photographic illustrations have been provided by the following and are reproduced here with their permission:

Fig. 33, British Museum.

Figs. 16, 62, 63 and 64, Cambridge University Committee for Aerial Photography.

Front cover and figs. 40, 48 and 58, Cambridge University Museum of Archaeology and Anthropology.

Fig. 11, Ministry of Defence.

All other photographs have been taken by the County Council's Photographic Unit (Ken Whitbread and Dave Stubbs).

The front cover shows a bronze head of Mercury from Sandy (copyright Cambridge University Museum of Archaeology and Anthropology; see also fig. 58). The title page illustration is a flagon found at Harrold (see G105); it is from an early 19th century watercolour, probably by Thomas Fisher, in the County Record Office (X254/88/219), and is reproduced by kind permission of the County Archivist. The vessel is now in Bedford Museum (acc. no. 3273).

Object illustrations by Pat Walsh.
Maps and diagrams by John Johnson, Angela Simco and Barry Wright.
Typeset by Beryl Bateman of Barber Typesetting in 9pt and 11pt Baskerville.
Layout by Jim Godfrey and John Johnson.

Bedfordshire County Council © 1984.
ISBN 0 907041 07 8

CONTENTS

ILLUSTRATIONS

Chapter 1

FROM ROMANCE TO RESEARCH

In his *Monumenta Britannica* of about 1666,[1] the antiquary John Aubrey spoke of "an urn, red like coral, with an inscription" from Sandy in Bedfordshire, a phrase which stands among the earliest references to Roman discoveries in the county. He wrote at a time when archaeology was in its infancy, and it is only with the benefit of subsequent research that we can recognise in his report a vessel of the fine red "samian" fabric stamped with the potter's name (such as figs. 29–31). During the 20th century, the discipline is often said to have "come of age", as techniques have improved and knowledge has increased, but further advances still take place year by year. As more information becomes available, so our understanding of the past evolves. Old ideas are superseded, and new approaches adopted. To summarise what is now known about Bedfordshire in Roman times involves bringing together a wide range of evidence, varying from those chance discoveries of centuries ago to the detailed conclusions of modern research.

The First Discoveries

In Aubrey's day, it was already well known that a Roman civilisation had existed across much of Europe, and that Britain had formed a province of the Roman Empire. The remains of many Roman buildings and monuments could still be seen in Italy and southern Europe, often preserved to a great height, but similar features were noticeably scarce in England. In a search for traces of Roman occupation, students of antiquity often turned to the ancient earthworks preserved in the landscape, and attempted to find in them signs of Roman workmanship. There are few areas in the country without a "Caesar's Camp", which usually (as with the example at Sandy) turns out to be a fortification of pre-Roman times.

1. *Colour-coated beaker, Sandy, G211. Scale 1:2*

There were similar problems in correctly identifying the artefacts that were found, particularly pottery. Finer, well-made vessels were usually thought to be Roman, while anything else was assumed to be more primitive and "British". This distinction was in many cases a correct one, but not invariably so. For example, a group of "Roman urns" from Sandy, illustrated in 1806,[2] includes one vessel which is clearly of early Saxon style. On the other hand, a vessel found in 1850, during the construction of the railway at

Sandy, was said to be Saxon, yet its description as an "elegant drinking cup: the ground dark and enamelled with a white flower, with a waving stalk, and trefoiled calyx, of a clover form"[3] enables it to be identified as a Roman beaker (fig. 1) now in Bedford Museum. Some finds made as late as 1887, near the old Charles Wells' brewery site in Horne Lane, Bedford,[4] were said to include Roman vessels, but these were in fact pottery fragments of medieval date.

At the opening of the 19th century, information about the Roman occupation of Bedfordshire was still sparse. Sandy was the best known site, with Aubrey's early record having been supplemented in the 18th century with references to "immense numbers of coins . . . . vases, urns, lachrymatories, lamps".[5] Coins were also prolific in the Dunstable area, even to the extent of a local dialect name — "madning-money" — being used to describe them.[6]

Otherwise, only a coin hoard from Totternhoe,[7] found in 1770, and amphorae from Wavendon Heath (now within Aspley Heath parish; fig. 2) and Maulden Moor[8] had appeared in the published accounts.

During the early nineteenth century, a number of new sites were identified, largely due to the work of Thomas Inskip of Shefford. Several of these produced many rich finds. Inskip's first recorded discovery was of a Roman cemetery at Shefford,[9] tracked down in 1826 after he found a coin in a load of gravel being used in road mending. He visited the pit from which it came and unearthed many complete pots, accompanied by vessels of glass and bronze, and many other finds. Assuming there must be a temple in the vicinity of the cemetery, Inskip searched for, and found, a building nearby, although what he uncovered is more likely to have been part of a Roman villa

2. *Amphora found on Wavendon Heath, G7. Scale 1:8.*

than a temple (see page 27).

Inskip also excavated two 1st century cremation burials at Stanfordbury,[10] in Southill parish, which contained many imported Roman objects, such as wine amphorae, samian pottery, and glass and bronze vessels. Thomas Inskip was a typical antiquary of his day. While he recognised the importance of the objects he was uncovering, he did not fully appreciate the information which a study of the different soil strata could have provided. Indeed, he seems not to have kept separate some of the finds from the different sites on which he worked,[11] and this has hindered more detailed analysis by modern researchers.

Of the generation of antiquaries who followed Inskip, some were professional men, such as James Wyatt and Thomas Gwyn Elger of Bedford, who in the middle and late 19th century recorded discoveries from gravel pits and development sites in and around the town. Others were landed gentry who took a keen interest in the antiquity of their estates and the surrounding countryside. Major W. Cooper Cooper, for example, published several reports of finds from the Toddington area, some of which he had been actively involved in excavating.

In 1882, William Thompson Watkin (better known for his work on Cheshire) published a paper entitled "Roman Bedfordshire"; this summarised much of the information then available, but also incorporated some of the misconceptions of earlier years. For example, Totternhoe medieval castle, and Maiden Bower Iron Age hillfort near Houghton Regis, were attributed to the Roman invaders. The finds which Watkin lists gives the impression that Roman remains were confined to the southern and eastern parts of the county (fig. 3a). Within just a few decades this picture was to change.

From Antiquary to Archaeologist

The late 19th century marked a turning point between the old-style antiquarian tradition and the modern discipline of archaeology. One of the key figures in this transition was Worthington G. Smith of Dunstable. His main interest was in the earliest (palaeolithic) remains of man in the Dunstable area, but in his regular visits to the small brick pits on the Chilterns he recorded finds of all periods. The results of his work, published chiefly in *Dunstable: Its History and Surroundings* (1904), demonstrated for the first

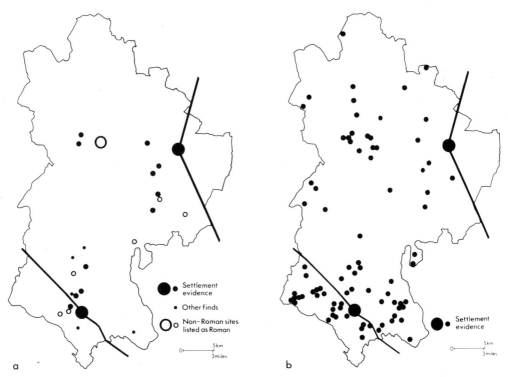

a

b

3. The state of the evidence, (a) according to W.T. Watkin, 1882 and (b) in 1945.

time that if an area were investigated in detail, and quarries and redevelopment sites monitored on a regular basis, then Roman finds were likely to turn up almost anywhere. However, he worked only in the south of the county. Thus the next survey of Roman Bedfordshire in the *Victoria County History* (1908) still reflected the bias towards the south and east in its distribution of sites.[12]

During the opening decades of this century, Frederick G. Gurney of Eggington contributed a great deal to the study through his work in the Leighton Buzzard area and elsewhere in south Bedfordshire.[13] Like Smith, he spent many hours searching fields and quarries for archaeological remains. However, not content merely to accumulate information, he tried to answer questions. For example, he noticed that Roman pottery could be picked up all over the boulder clay ridges of Eggington and Stanbridge, but not in the valleys below. To check this initial impression he concentrated his search on the valleys: "In the wet bottom occupied by the old village greens and some small fields. I have never found a scrap [of pottery], though I have searched the tiny stream here and every piece of ploughland."[14] As a result he was able to conclude with some confidence that Roman settlements in that area were indeed to be found on the hilltops, rather than in the poorly-drained valleys where the present villages are located (see Gazetteer Map F).

The imbalance towards the south of the county began to be corrected during the 1930s, mainly through the work of F.W. Kuhlicke. His activities with the Bedford Modern School Field Club, and the infectious enthusiasm which he passed on to many of his pupils, enabled him to build up the collections of the Bedford Modern School Museum (even-

tually to become the present Bedford Museum), and to accumulate records of many new discoveries. By 1945, the difference between south and north was considerably less marked (fig. 3b).

Of all the Roman settlements known in the county today (see figs. 7 and 8), almost two-thirds have been discovered since 1945. This is due to a widening interest in archaeology, to the increased numbers of both individuals and societies involved in archaeological work, and to the greater level of archaeological monitoring of development schemes, roadworks and quarries. Particular advances have been made through the method of detailed field-walking, in which an area of arable land is thoroughly searched after ploughing for scatters of finds brought to the surface from the buried sites beneath. The use of aerial photography has revealed settlements and field systems through variations in crop growth. Rescue recording in advance of development provides much detailed evidence which continues to add to the picture.

No map of archaeological finds can ever be said to be complete. New discoveries are always being made, and the overall picture is constantly changing. We have seen how the accumulation of information has accelerated over the last two or three hundred years; while the next few centuries are unlikely to produce quite the same quantity of new sites, they will no doubt shed fresh light on areas as yet obscure. In the meantime, the following pages will look beyond the dots on the map, the brief notes in antiquarian journals, the stray finds in museums and the reports from modern excavations, and present a 1980s view of Bedfordshire and its people in Roman times.

Chapter 2

BEFORE THE CONQUEST

When the Roman legions invaded Britain in AD 43, they did not come to a sparsely populated and primitive country. Julius Caesar's description, written in the 1st century BC, of woad-covered Britons terrifying the enemy in battle,[1] has coloured the popular image of the pre-Roman inhabitants; but warfare was only one aspect of their lives among many. For the most part, their priority was to meet the demands of everyday life — growing crops, raising stock, and trading the surplus for those goods which could not be made at home. Many features of their way of life survived throughout the years of Roman rule; a brief survey of this Iron Age background will therefore help our understanding of what was to follow after the Roman invasion.

During later prehistory, the population of lowland England grew as improvements in technology led to greater agricultural productivity. This increase in population had a number of effects. Shortage of the best quality land led to the clearance of woodland and the establishment of settlements on some of the heavier clay soils. Farmsteads and their fields were defined much more clearly with extensive ditch systems, reflecting the need to mark the boundaries of land tenure. Hillforts and other defensive earthworks were constructed to guard against encroachments by neighbours, and to serve as tribal centres of commerce, administration and religious ceremony.

Along with the increase in population came a high degree of social organisation. The construction of hillforts (of which the best Bedfordshire examples are Maiden Bower near Houghton Regis, and Caesar's Camp and Galley Hill at Sandy) required a central authority with sufficient power to raise a labour force, and to provide in return protection and "central services". The importance of defining territory is emphasised by the earthwork known as Dray's Ditches, which cuts across the Icknield Way north of Luton. This probably served as a major boundary, but was no doubt also used to control traffic and perhaps as a barrier for collecting tolls.[2]

Arrival of the "Belgae"

The century and a half before AD 43 was a period of great change for the south-east of England. Julius Caesar, in describing his military expeditions to Britain in 55 and 54 BC, wrote of a people known as the "Belgae", who inhabited north-eastern France, and who had crossed over into Britain.[3] The effect of this movement can be detected in broad terms in south-east England, in the development of new pottery styles (fig. 4)[4] and the adoption of new forms of burial.

Julius Caesar's accounts also give us our earliest historical references to the names of British tribal groups and their leaders.[5] In 54 BC he defeated Cassivellaunus, who had been entrusted with the overall command of the British resistance, at his stronghold which may have been at Wheathampstead, 5 miles (8 kilometres) north-east of St Albans.[6] The treaty which Caesar imposed involved the payment of tribute, the requisition of hostages, and the agreement of

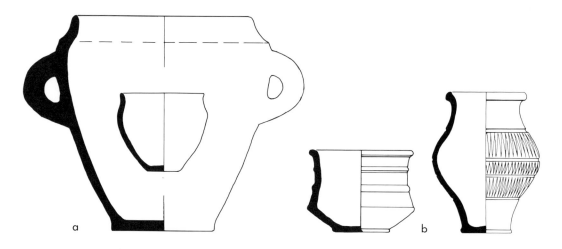

4. Changing Iron Age pottery styles: (a) pre-Belgic vessels, Harrold; (b) Belgic vessels, Felmersham and Kempston (see G125). Scale 1:4.

Cassivellaunus not to molest his eastern neighbours, the Trinovantes. Cassivellaunus' territory, which was later identified with the tribe of the Catuvellauni, was located north of the Thames, mainly in what is now Hertfordshire. The extreme southern part of Bedfordshire may also have fallen under his jurisdiction.

Tribal differences are difficult to detect in the archaeological record but the distribution of coins does help when other evidence is lacking. Coins were first introduced from the continent towards the end of the 2nd century BC, and local versions began to be produced during the early 1st century BC. Towards the end of that century, under the influence of contact with the Roman Empire, coins began to be inscribed with the names of kings, the first in the Catuvellaunian area being that of Tasciovanus. He ruled from *c.* 20 BC to *c.* AD 5/10, and was almost certainly responsible for establishing the new tribal capital at Verulamium, near St Albans.[7] His coins, in bronze as well as gold and silver, are known in quantity throughout Bedfordshire, demonstrating that Catuvellaunian influence had expanded as far north as

the Ouse valley by the opening of the 1st century AD at the latest. Even more numerous in Bedfordshire are the coins of Tasciovanus' successor, Cunobelinus. This ruler has traditionally been assumed to have been Tasciovanus' son, and therefore a Catuvellaunian. Recent research has however raised the possibility that he was in fact leader of the Trinovantes, based at Camulodunum (Colchester), who took over the Catuvellaunian territory in *c.* AD 10.[8] During the first half of the 1st century AD, Cunobelinus' empire thus covered a large area north of the Thames.

The Belgic expansion across Bedfordshire did not involve the total expulsion of the original inhabitants. There are no signs of widespread violent destruction of the earlier Iron Age settlements, although so few have been excavated that it is difficult to generalise. However, there is evidence of some displacement of population, and this can best be demonstrated by looking at the relationship between Belgic and pre-Belgic settlements (fig. 5). It can be seen that there are very few sites where a settlement of the earlier Iron Age lies directly beneath

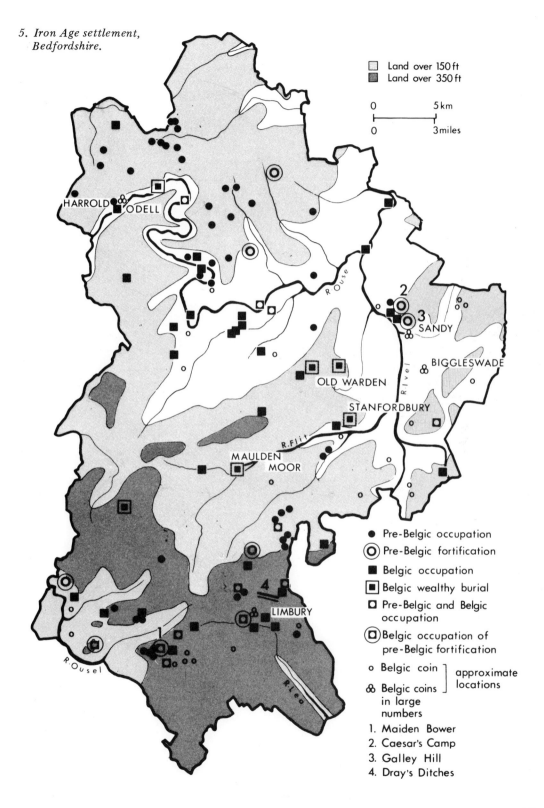

5. *Iron Age settlement, Bedfordshire.*

Land over 150 ft
Land over 350 ft

0   5 km
0   3 miles

HARROLD ODELL

R. Ouse

2
3 SANDY

BIGGLESWADE

R. Ivel

OLD WARDEN

STANFORDBURY

R. Flit

MAULDEN MOOR

LIMBURY

4

1

R. Ousel

R. Lea

● Pre-Belgic occupation
◉ Pre-Belgic fortification
■ Belgic occupation
▣ Belgic wealthy burial
◘ Pre-Belgic and Belgic occupation
◉ Belgic occupation of pre-Belgic fortification
○ Belgic coin   } approximate
⚮ Belgic coins   } locations
   in large
   numbers

1. Maiden Bower
2. Caesar's Camp
3. Galley Hill
4. Dray's Ditches

one of Belgic date. This suggests that the arrival of Belgic characteristics (for example, pottery styles) was not just due to the local population adopting ideas from their Belgic neighbours. If that had been the case, one would expect settlements to have continued in existence on the same spot, while the pottery styles gradually developed Belgic characteristics. Although some indigenous Iron Age sites occasionally produce pottery with some Belgic features, and *vice versa*, on the whole there is an abrupt change between the two styles.

Belgic settlements seem to occur almost exclusively on the better soil in the county: along the River Lea and on the chalk uplands, on the high quality land of the Ivel and Flit valleys, in the Ouse valley, and across the Ouse-Nene watershed in the tributary valleys of the River Nene. In north-west Bedfordshire, where detailed survey work has been carried out, Belgic occupation hardly ever occurs away from the valleys, with their well-drained gravel deposits, although earlier Iron Age sites are quite common on the clay hills. The implication is that the Belgic population spread northwards through Bedfordshire, taking over the more favourable areas but not occupying the poorer land. The original inhabitants were either totally absorbed into the new population (perhaps as slaves), or just squeezed out on to the less fertile land where the earlier settlements may have remained undisturbed. This situation was frozen in time by the arrival of the occupying Roman power.

Where Belgic settlements were established on totally fresh ground, the earlier Iron Age sites which they may have replaced can sometimes be identified. For example, just north of Harrold, evidence of a pre-Belgic settlement was salvaged during gravel extraction in the 1950s.[9] Traces of several houses were found,

along with pits and ditches containing pottery of indigenous Iron Age style (see fig. 4a). A few vessels showed some Belgic-type features, indicating that this settlement lasted until Belgic influences were beginning to be felt in the area. No evidence was found as to why the settlement was abandoned. A few hundred yards away to the south-east, in the parish of Odell, investigations took place on another site between 1974 and 1978, also in advance of gravel extraction, but this time achieving almost complete excavation (see page 24).[10] This farmstead began its life at the end of the 1st century BC, and displayed only Belgic characteristics from the start. This is consistent with the arrival of a new population which established new settlements, and gradually excluded or absorbed the earlier inhabitants, causing the abandonment of their sites.

The Eve of Invasion

By the time of the Roman conquest, the Bedfordshire area was fairly densely settled, both by Belgic newcomers and by survivors of the original Iron Age population. This settlement took the form of large numbers of farmsteads, occurring in most areas of the county, consisting of a group of dwellings, surrounded by enclosed fields and wider areas of pasture, and occupied perhaps by a small group of related families. There is evidence, in the form of richly furnished cremation burials, of the strong aristocratic element in Belgic society. The cremated remains were accompanied by offerings, presumably with the intention of providing for the needs of the deceased in the next life. The greater the wealth and social standing of the dead person, the richer the offering. From this, it can be seen that much of the wealth and power in pre-Roman Bedfordshire was concentrated in the Ivel valley.

From Stanfordbury,[11] in Southill parish, two burial "vaults" dug up by Thomas Inskip in 1832 and 1834, although probably dating from just after the Roman invasion, fall firmly within the Belgic tradition of wealthy burial. They were floored with rough tiles, and were first discovered when some agricultural drains were being dug. The grave furniture included many items imported from the Roman Empire, including several wine amphorae, bronze and glass vessels, and many red samian ware pots from Gaul. A tripod, spits, and iron firedogs stood duty for feasts beyond the grave, while gaming counters, beads and bracelets provided for entertainment and personal adornment.

Further north at Old Warden, a cremation was accompanied by two lathe-turned vases of Kimmeridge shale, and an iron-bound bucket;[12] a finely decorated mirror found during the excavation of the Warden railway tunnel probably came from another such burial in the same parish.[13] It is probably no coinci-dence that the Ivel valley has also produced the largest number of gold and silver Belgic coins to be found anywhere in the county.

The clear impression given by these rich cremation burials, as by others in south-east England, is that contact with the Roman world was growing ever stronger. While perhaps maintaining a token hostility to the Roman Empire, those who could afford to do so would unhesitatingly acquire, and value, Roman goods. As demand from Britain increased so did the level of trade and exchange. Part of that exchange involved the entry into Britain of traders and merchants from the continent, and no doubt the nature of Britain and its inhabitants, which had been almost a closed book to Caesar a century earlier, became more familiar in the Roman world, and, more significantly, in Rome itself. The time was ripe for Roman interest to be resumed in the land "beyond the Ocean", and it required little for that interest to be stirred into action.

Chapter 3

THE ROMAN INVASION

When Cunobelinus died in *c*. AD 40, his large kingdom was divided between his sons, Caratacus and Togodumnus, who resumed the expansionist policies of their father. They turned their attention southward to the lands of the Atrebates in the Sussex area (see fig. 6); Verica, the Atrebatic king, was expelled and fled to Rome, appealing to the emperor Claudius for assistance. He was not the first deposed British ruler since the days of Caesar to follow this route, but his appeal could not be dismissed quite so easily as those of his predecessors. The Atrebates had been allies of Rome since the days when the emperor Augustus may have made a treaty with them in *c*. 15 BC. Their defeat was a serious blow to Roman prestige, and ought not to go unavenged.

This incident provided the final excuse for Roman involvement in Britain. Claudius had as yet no military triumph to his name, and the conquest of a new province was an attractive goal. When that province held out the hope of profit which Britain offered in her mineral and agricultural wealth, the attraction was irresistible.

In the spring of AD 43, four Roman legions, and several units of auxiliary troops, crossed the channel under the command of Aulus Plautius. Their target was the Catuvellaunian/Trinovantian empire, and in this they had the support and encouragement of those tribes which had borne the brunt of decades of aggression. The decisive battle took place near the mouth of the river Medway. Togodumnus was killed, and Caratacus escaped to the west. The news was sent to Claudius, who came in person to lead the triumphal entry into Camulodunum, the native capital, and to receive the surrender of those rulers who had not fled.

From a military base at Camulodunum, three of the four legions fanned out to complete the occupation of lowland England. Legio II under the future emperor Vespasian headed west, leaving evidence of its route in a number of sacked hillforts, such as Hod Hill and Maiden Castle in Dorset. Legio IX Hispana moved north, eventually to a base at Lincoln. Between these two, Legio XIV Gemina advanced north-west towards the midlands. In the wake of the legions, military engineers laid out the great supply roads, and forts were established to garrison the conquered territory, and to guard against local uprisings. By AD 47, the Roman advance was consolidated on the line of the Trent and Severn.

Conquest without Resistance

Evidence of this first military advance through Bedfordshire, as through the rest of lowland England, is difficult to find. No military sites have been identified in the county, and few, if any, Iron Age settlements show signs of warfare or violent destruction. That Legio XIV passed through the south-west of the county is suggested by the line of its supply road, Watling Street. A fort at Verulamium (St Albans), close to the earlier Catuvellaunian capital, lay on this road,[1] and there may have been one near Fenny Stratford at the site which was to develop into the town of Magiovinium.[2] Midway between these two, we might expect a fort or other military post on

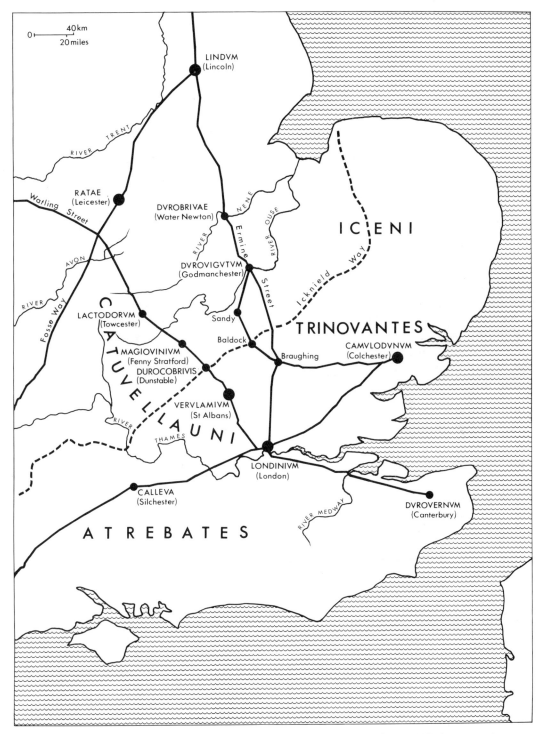

6. *South-East England: Iron Age tribes and the Roman Conquest (a simplified map to show features mentioned in the text).*

17

the site of Dunstable, known in Roman times as Durocobrivis.[3] None has yet been found, in spite of extensive excavations in the town over recent years.[4]

East of Bedfordshire, Ermine Street (the modern A10 and A14) reflects the line of advance of Legio IX. A road leading from Ermine Street links Braughing with Godmanchester (almost certainly known as Durovigutum) via Baldock and Sandy, all of which developed into Roman settlements. This route takes in the Ivel valley, the home of the local Catuvellaunian aristocracy; perhaps it was associated with a military post at Sandy, set up to discourage local resistance. The road has been dated by excavations at Godmanchester to very early in the Roman occupation.[5]

Several reasons lie behind the apparent absence of any serious military conflict on a local level. The military strength of the Catuvellauni had been centralised under the control of the tribal rulers. A surrender by the central authority of the tribe, and the disbanding of its troops, embodied within it the surrender of the whole tribe, including its lesser aristocracy and the men they commanded. With that surrender, political control was in the hands of the Roman invaders, and the *fait accompli*, reinforced by the presence of the occasional garrison, seems to have been accepted with little or no local resistance. It is clear from the mid-1st century cremations at Stanfordbury,[6] and 1st century burials at Shefford[7] and Biggleswade,[8] that the native aristocracy in Bedfordshire, at least in the Ivel valley, retained their wealth and status after the conquest.

It must not be forgotten that the vast majority of the population were tied to the land for their livelihood. To interrupt the cycle of the farming year in order to harrass the new conquerors might well mean starvation through loss of crops. It was also in the interests of the Roman authorities that the native agricultural economy be disrupted as little as possible. It was on the native farms that the troops and administrators would depend for their own food supply, and they could not afford to indulge in the unnecessary destruction of rural communities which were not proving a military threat. No doubt the average Catuvellaunian had become all too familiar with the power struggles among the masters of his own and other tribes and the Roman invasion was viewed as just another change of government.

While the military forces pushed further west and north, the south-east part of the province Britannia settled down to reap the benefits of its new status. However, the immediate impact of the Roman occupation on the way of life of the Iron Age rural population was slight. Although the old tribal political structure was soon absorbed into the new Roman administration, changes in the standard of living were scarcely felt for years, if not decades. Many features of life — the agricultural technology, styles of pottery and metalwork, methods of building construction — continued as they had been in pre-Roman times, and were only gradually influenced and altered by new Roman ideas.

The Boudican Rebellion

The slowness of the "Romanisation" process was probably related to the major rebellion of AD 60/61, led by the famous Boudica, of the Iceni tribe of the Norfolk area. Her husband Prasutagus had been a "client king", who was allowed a degree of independence in return for supporting the Roman invaders. On his death, the authorities seized his property in such a brutal manner that it sparked off an uprising which spread across East Anglia. The new Roman town at Camulodunum was sacked and burnt, followed by London and Verulamium. The rebels were eventually routed by Legio XIV, under the command of the governor, Suetonius Paulinus, hastily recalled from campaigns in north Wales.

Literary accounts[9] give a graphic representation of violence and atrocities by many thousands of rebels; more reliable is the archaeological evidence from the three towns, which shows that they were almost completely destroyed. A major fire at Godmanchester at this time can probably also be attributed to this uprising.[10] The countryside at large, as at the original conquest, does not seem to have been so drastically affected. The violence was directed against the tangible signs of the Roman presence — public buildings and Roman-style town houses, for example. Few rural settlements were as yet so distinguished. For several years after the rebellion was put down, it seems there were few natives in the affected area who dared identify themselves too closely with the occupying power. But with changes in the personnel of government, security was eventually restored. The towns were rebuilt, and the rural communities began to acquire whatever aspects of Roman civilisation they could afford. The sons of leading Britons were educated after the Roman manner, and it became fashionable to display all the outward trappings of a Roman way of life.

The area which is now Bedfordshire was a small, and not particularly significant part of the Roman province of Britain. While its history was firmly rooted in its Iron Age past, it was influenced and moulded by four hundred years of Roman rule. The following chapters look at some of the details of life under that rule.

Chapter 4

SETTLEMENTS IN THE LANDSCAPE

The Roman occupation of Britain was not marked by large numbers of immigrant settlers. The newcomers were mainly military personnel or administrative staff, many of whom stayed only to serve their term of office. There were also merchants, continuing the pre-invasion links between Britain and the continent, and skilled craftsmen, setting up workshops to take advantage of the rapidly expanding market. For an analogy from modern history we may perhaps take the British occupation of India. British soldiers and administrative officers were familiar figures, as were British business men, but there was no mass popular emigration, as there was to Australia and New Zealand, or to north America.

The settlements of Roman Britain were occupied, and the land farmed, by the indigenous population and their descendants. The pattern of those settlements therefore has its origin in the Iron Age landscape, moulded only slightly by the effects of the Roman occupation. This chapter will look at the Roman landscape of Bedfordshire, and at the different types of settlement to be found in it.

Settlement and Geology

The distribution map of known Roman settlements in Bedfordshire (figs. 7 and 8) has to be treated with some caution.[1] The large numbers plotted in the north-west and south of the county, for example, do not necessarily demonstrate a higher population in Roman times, but they do reveal the areas where much archaeological work has been carried out. The discovery of sites is governed to a great extent by recent land-use history. An area of land completely given over to pasture will effectively conceal its buried sites, while on arable land evidence is regularly turned up by the plough. Extensive redevelopment schemes or mineral extraction tend to reveal yet more material, and will often allow access for archaeological investigation which would otherwise be unavailable.

Not all the settlements shown were necessarily inhabited at the same time. Some may have been abandoned during the period, while others were established on new ground. Many small settlement shifts probably occurred, as farmsteads were relocated, and the picture was by no means static throughout the four hundred years of the Roman occupation.

Clearly there are few parts of the county where some Roman evidence has not been recovered, but there are signs that some areas were more popular, and populous, than others. An important factor governing the location of settlements was the nature of the land, which is itself largely determined by the underlying geology. By looking at the distribution of settlements in relation to the geology and topography, a pattern begins to emerge. For example, there is a concentration of settlements along the gravels of the river valleys, and on the chalky soils of the Chiltern hills in the south.

Although it used to be thought that the heavier clay soils of lowland England were not cleared of woodland for cultivation until the Saxon period, survey work, particularly over the last twenty years, has shown that this was not the case. In the north-west of the county, Roman sites have been found all over the chalky boulder clay uplands. The same is true in the Leighton Buzzard area, where settlements have been identified at regular intervals along the boulder clay capped ridges. This particular clay has a reasonable pebble content which made cultivation and drainage practicable. As a result, evidence of Roman occupation is likely to be found wherever it occurs, which includes much of the higher ground in the county.

There are, however, some parts of the county where settlement evidence is sparse, or totally absent. One of the largest gaps on the map can be seen to the south-west of Bedford, in the Marston vale, where there is a large expanse of Oxford clay. Such scarcity of evidence is sometimes due to the lack of detailed archaeological survey or because extensive mineral extraction, with massive earth-moving machinery, has destroyed sites without their being noticed. On the other hand, in the 19th and early 20th centuries, the Marston vale was dotted with many small hand-dug brick pits; it is most unlikely that archaeological remains, if uncovered, would have gone entirely undetected by the labourer, and that some, at least, would not have come to the attention of one of several antiquaries working in the Bedford area at the time. Furthermore, where field-work has been carried out in recent years on similar soils outside the county, the scarcity of sites is still noticeable.[2] The weight of evidence is therefore beginning to indicate that the Oxford clay areas of the county really were largely unsettled in the Roman period. This was almost certainly due to the very poor drainage properties and heavy consistency of the soil.

Near Leighton Buzzard, the lack of Roman finds at the foot of the hills was first recognised by F.G. Gurney (see page 10). In this area, the wet valley bottoms lie on poorly-drained gault clay, which is much less easily worked than the boulder clay of the hills. This gault clay deposit lies between the greensand ridge and the Chilterns, running roughly south-west to north-east across the county. Wherever Roman sites occur in this vale, they tend to be either on small pockets of gravel alongside streams, or on isolated patches of boulder clay capping. As a geological deposit, gault clay does not seem to have been favoured for settlement.

Another large blank area on the map occurs around Woburn, to the east of Magiovinium. It is not yet possible to say whether this gap is due to a real absence of settlement or to other factors, such as the land-use history of the area. For example, Woburn Park amounts to more than 2000 acres (800 hectares) of non-arable land, and much of the agricultural land around it has been permanent pasture until very recently. On the other hand, the area does have its own particular geological peculiarities, in that it lies on a deposit of decalcified boulder clay. This clay gives rise to poorly-drained acid soils which were probably fairly unproductive agriculturally and therefore did not encourage settlement.

Farmstead and Villa

The social hierarchy of Britain during the Roman period was rooted in that which existed in the late Iron Age. The families which held political power before the conquest, except perhaps those whom the new masters adjudged a threat to security, went on to play a part in the new administration of the province. Each tribe, or *civitas*, had its own council of magistrates, based in the *civitas* capital, which was responsible for ensuring local conformity to the wishes

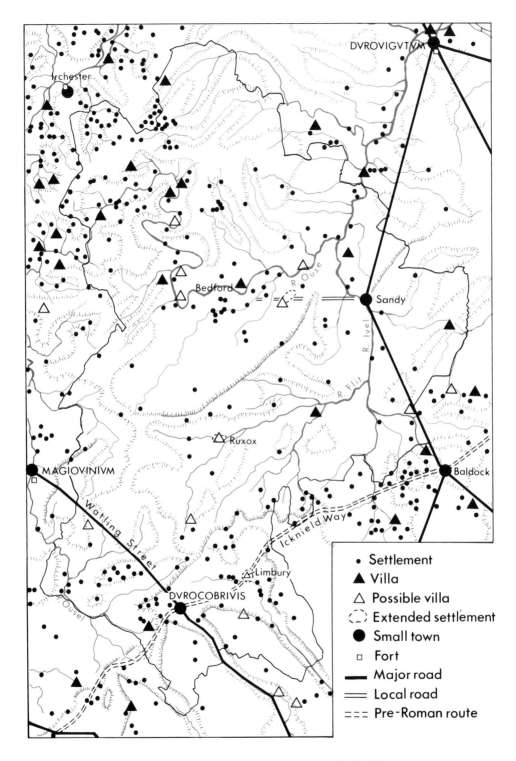

Irchester

DVROVIGVTVM

Bedford

R. Ouse

R. Ivel

Sandy

R. Flit

Ruxox

MAGIOVINIVM

Watling Street

Baldock

R. Ousel

Icknield Way

Limbury

DVROCOBRIVIS

Settlement
▲ Villa
△ Possible villa
⬭ Extended settlement
● Small town
□ Fort
▬ Major road
═ Local road
╌ Pre-Roman route

7. Roman settlement in Bedfordshire: relief and drainage.

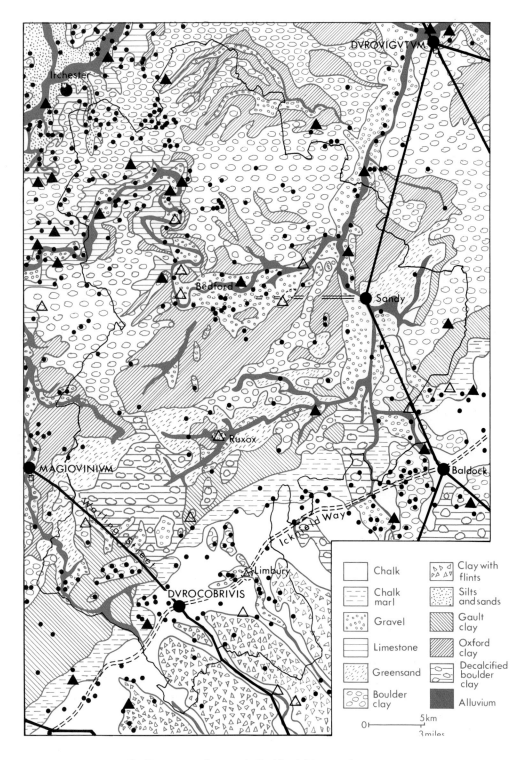

Chalk
Chalk marl
Gravel
Limestone
Greensand
Boulder clay
Clay with flints
Silts and sands
Gault clay
Oxford clay
Decalcified boulder clay
Alluvium

0   5km
0   3miles

8. Roman settlement in Bedfordshire: geology.

23

and demands of the imperial government. Verulamium, as the *civitas* capital of the Catuvellauni, provided the tribal administration for the Bedfordshire area.

It is likely (by analogy with continental Europe) that each tribe was further subdivided into administrative units called *pagi,* which again may have been based on pre-Roman arrangements. There was possibly a council of magistrates, or lesser officials, over each *pagus.* The area of land covered by a *pagus* is unknown, although small towns probably acted as administrative centres for the countryside around them. Within Bedfordshire, Durocobrivis and Sandy may have served this function, while some areas are more likely to have looked towards settlements outside the modern county boundary, such as Magiovinium, Irchester (near Rushden, Northamptonshire) or Baldock (north Hertfordshire).

Social hierarchy is reflected in the settlements of Roman Bedfordshire by the different standards of living which can be detected in the material remains. The vast majority were single farmsteads, with undistinguished dwellings and farm buildings, set in a group of roughly rectangular fields. The most completely recorded example of this kind of settlement in Bedfordshire is that at Odell (fig. 9; see also page 14). Established at the end of the 1st century BC at the time of the Belgic expansion through Bedfordshire, its layout consisted of a number of rectangular fields on each side of a trackway, with a habitation enclosure containing two circular timber houses. The occupants cannot have been more numerous than two or three (probably related) families, sharing the same accommodation. A mixed agriculture was practised, both stock and arable. Crops were grown

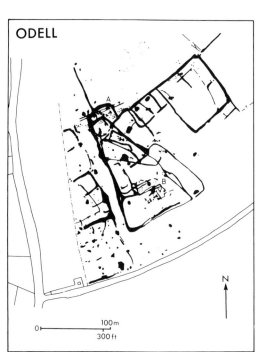

9. *Odell: composite plan of the excavated features (G187). A and B are the two settlement centres shown on fig. 10.*

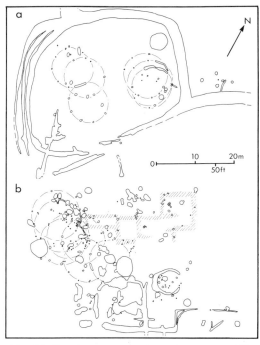

10. *Odell: the two settlement centres. The earlier farmstead site A was replaced by that at B at the end of the 1st century AD.*

in the fields near the farmstead and were protected from straying animals by boundary ditches. Nearby land provided pasture for cattle and sheep.

The original layout of the Odell farmstead was unaffected by the conquest, and was not substantially changed until the end of the 1st century AD. Even then, the alteration only involved a shift in the location of the dwelling houses and farm buildings (fig. 10); the field pattern remained more or less the same, undergoing only piecemeal alterations, such as the sub-division or enlargement of fields. Circular houses continued in use, following the Iron Age fashion, although in the latter part of the farmstead's life a rectangular building was constructed which probably provided a reasonable standard of accommodation. Other signs of the influence of the Roman occupation can be seen in a stone-built drying oven (see fig. 19) and stone-lined wells.

While few other Roman farmstead sites have been excavated in the county, and none so extensively as Odell, it is likely that most of them followed the same overall pattern. Near the River Ouse at Wyboston in Roxton parish, a compact group of fields, recorded as cropmarks on aerial photographs, was investigated in the 1950s, also in advance of gravel extraction. The two circles on the aerial photograph (fig. 11) were Belgic round houses; by the 2nd century the dwelling area seems to have shifted to the south-west (bottom left of the photograph), where a possible drying oven was recorded. At Flitwick, rescue excavations on the site of the Manor Way housing development uncovered a 2nd century drying oven within a square ditched enclosure,[3] probably all that could be identified of a small farming community.

While Bedfordshire can offer little to

11. Belgic and Roman farmstead, Wyboston, G206. (Crown copyright reserved).

match luxury villas such as Lullingstone (Kent), Woodchester (Gloucestershire) or Latimer (Buckinghamshire), it is clear that there were a number of sites whose inhabitants enjoyed a higher standard of living than those of the farmsteads described above. The features which reflect this higher standard are mosaic or tessellated pavements, painted wall-plaster, and hypocausts (underfloor heating systems) or bath-houses. These sites may not have equalled the wealth of the Cotswold and Chiltern villas, but they were almost certainly of a higher social status than the much more numerous farmsteads of native type.

The only site in Bedfordshire which clearly comes near the standard of wealthy villas elsewhere has been found at Totternhoe. Stone rubble ploughed up in 1954 betrayed its existence, and some excavations were later carried out by the Manshead Archaeological Society. Its 4th century plan consisted of a series of rooms arranged round three sides of a courtyard (fig. 12). Some of the rooms were floored with mosaic and tessellated

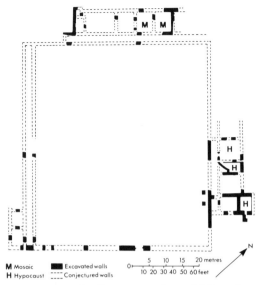

M Mosaic ■ Excavated walls
H Hypocaust ---- Conjectured walls

0 5 10 15 20 metres
0 10 20 30 40 50 60 feet

N

12. Courtyard villa, Totternhoe, G265; after Matthews, 1963.

pavements, and there was a bath block. The fragment of mosaic shown in figure 13 was also found at Totternhoe, probably in the last century. Its pattern is very similar to one of the mosaics uncovered in 1954,[4] and it almost certainly came from the same building. Clearly the owner was a person of some importance; as the villa lies only about 12 miles northwest of Verulamium, it may even have been the country residence of some dignitary whose business or civic responsibilities required him to live close to the tribal capital.

At Newnham, just east of Bedford, a villa-type building was excavated in 1972-75. Part of the site had been quarried away during the 1950s, and the rest of it was to be similarly destroyed. It had begun life in the early Roman period, when the pottery was still very like that used in the Belgic Iron Age. At first a rectangular timber building was set in the middle of a group of fields. These were later totally reorganised, and the whole establishment surrounded by a rectangular ditch. Stone buildings were

constructed, in one of which (probably a bath-house) survived the very bottom of an under-floor heating system (see figs. 14 and 15). This building seems to have been altered at some time, as the stoking area for the hypocaust was located within what would normally have been a living room. The stone foundations were removed sometime after the Roman period, and destructive ploughing was carried out during the Middle Ages, but the quality of the broken pottery and the fragmentary remains of painted wall-plaster show that a fair degree of luxury was enjoyed by the occupants. However, the surrounding fields, and the well-used appearance of the cobbled yard next to the buildings, demonstrate that villas were working farms as well as comfortable country houses. Some of them may also have carried out certain industrial func-

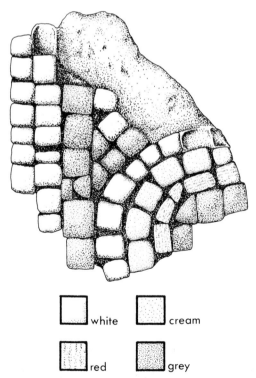

□ white   □ cream
▨ red   ▨ grey

13. Mosaic fragment from the Totternhoe villa. Scale 3:4.

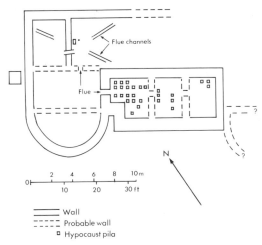

14. *Bath-house, Newnham, G13.*

Wall
Probable wall
□ Hypocaust pila

tions, such as iron-smelting (see page 48).

Some villas have been identified by discoveries made during small-scale excavations, or in the course of redevelopment. At Tempsford,[5] trial excavations on a site which had been discovered through ploughing produced fragments of mosaic tesserae and marble, but no building was located; at Radwell, Felmersham,[6] observation of a gravel quarry revealed fragments of window glass, and flue tiles from a heating system, which presumably came from a villa nearby; near the Roman cemetery at Shefford,[7] a small fragment of hypocaust, previously identified by Thomas Inskip as a "temple" (see page 8), was recorded in 1940 before new school buildings were erected.

Other villa sites can be conjectured from 19th century accounts. At Sheepwalk Hill in Toddington parish, an Anglo-Saxon skeleton was found "lying on a bed of concrete four to six inches thick, and not less than nine feet square". This must have been earlier in date than the skeleton, and a Roman mortar floor would have seemed very like concrete to a 19th century workman.[8] In 1857, a stone-lined well, discovered during gravel extraction at Biddenham,[9] was found to

15. *Remains of hypocaust, Newnham, viewed from the south.*

contain fragments of sculptured stone, including a human torso and a bird, and may betray the existence of an otherwise unknown villa in the vicinity (see fig. 56).

Sometimes the presence of a villa is revealed by scatters of finds in the ploughsoil. For example, in the Ouse valley at Carlton, dressed stone and roof and flue tiles indicate a buried building.[10] Occasionally a villa is suggested only by regular cropmarks, for example at Astwick (see fig. 65)[11] and Pavenham (fig. 16).

Most if not all of the villa sites in the county are likely to have belonged to members of the native aristocracy, who clearly enjoyed a higher level of wealth than the population as a whole, as they had already done in pre-Roman times. There is a marked correlation between the distribution of the wealthiest pre-Roman finds in the county and that of richer villa sites (see fig. 5). For example, the Ivel valley has produced large numbers of gold and silver Iron Age coins, and the rich cremation burials at Stan-

16. *Possible villa site, Pavenham, G192 (Cambridge University Collection: copyright reserved).*

fordbury[12] and Old Warden[13] (see page 15); in the Roman period it is noted for the settlement at Sandy (see page 30) and the villa and wealthy cemetery at Shefford. From Limbury, where an extensive area of occupation is centred on a possible villa,[14] quantities of pre-Roman coins have also been reported.[15] In the Flitwick/Maulden area, a cremation burial accompanied by an amphora and samian pottery[16] may have belonged to the same family group that established the wealthy settlement at Ruxox.[17]

As Bedfordshire had no other great natural resources from which an Iron Age ruler could derive his wealth, control over the land itself must have been the basis on which the power of the aristocracy was founded. It is surely no co-incidence that the most valuable agricultural land in Bedfordshire today lies in the Ivel and Flit valleys, where the aristocratic presence can so clearly be seen. How this control of land was administered can only be conjectured. Perhaps there was a similar arrangement to that of medieval England, when all land was technically owned by the king, but tenanted by others in return for dues and services, who in their turn had sub-tenants, and so on down through society. At a local level, the lord of each medieval manor had control over the tenants of his manorial estate, and received dues from them, in the form of goods or services. It is tempting to see in the villas the Roman equivalent of the medieval manorial centres, with the surrounding farmsteads being dependent settlements bound by some form of tenancy or other obligations.

Villas formed a very small proportion of all settlements, which is only to be expected if they represent the rural homes of the aristocracy. They also lie on better land, usually in the main river valleys, or at the head of tributary valleys. Their exact number is not known, although where much field-work has been done in the upper Ouse valley their distribution suggests that a villa site may be expected at every few miles along the valley side. This spacing is very similar to that of the modern villages, and of their medieval predecessors (fig. 17), and it would not be unreasonable in this area to expect to find a villa in every parish. This does not necessarily mean that all the medieval parishes in this area have their origin in Roman estates. It is likely, however, that the natural features which serve as boundaries today (the River Ouse, for example, or the ridgeway separating the Ouse and Nene valleys) also did so in Roman times.

Analysing the distribution and location of villa sites enables some conjecture as to where other villas might be found. For example, there is no known villa north-west of Bedford in the Clapham/ Oakley area, but crushed brick recently discovered in the original mortar of the Saxo-Norman tower at Clapham church points to a source of Roman brick or tile in the vicinity.[18]

At the southern end of the Ivel valley, a lost villa at Arlesey may be represented by the large quantity of samian vessels recovered from the parish;[19] the chalk marl deposits would have been a suitable location. Near Leighton Buzzard, around the edge of the Ousel basin, the villa at Totternhoe, and another possible one at Heath and Reach,[20] lie at the upper end of tributary valleys; a further example may turn up at the head of another tributary valley, in the northern part of Houghton Regis parish (see Gazetteer Map F).[21]

Town and Village

To a citizen of Rome, the very foundation of civilised life was the town. In late Iron Age Britain, some of the tribal

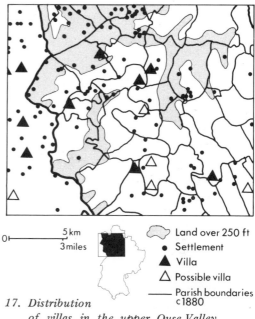

17. *Distribution of villas in the upper Ouse Valley.*

Legend: Land over 250 ft · Settlement ▲ Villa △ Possible villa — Parish boundaries c1880

centres such as Verulamium and Camulodunum had developed urban functions, as places of administration, trade and industry, but the 1st century invaders were unlikely to have recognised them as towns in the Roman sense. The upper classes in Roman society were primarily town dwellers, with country estates, run by bailiffs, providing both an income and an occasional "holiday home". In imposing a Roman administration on Britain, this was the arrangement which was expected to develop. To some extent it did, in that those native leaders who began to play a part in the local government of the province were required to live in the town in which they were magistrates. But there were still large areas with no towns, in the sense of settlements with public buildings, surrounded by walls or other defences. Within Bedfordshire, the emphasis was always predominantly rural, with very few settlements showing signs of a concentration of population. Only two places can perhaps be classed as small towns —

Dunstable and Sandy.

The modern town of Dunstable owes its existence to the foundation of a medieval borough in c. 1119 by Henry I.[22] However, the existence of an earlier settlement had been suspected as early as the 17th century, because of the large numbers of Roman coins which could be picked up in the area (see page 8).[23] A further pointer was provided by references in the Antonine Itinerary (a road book giving routes and the towns along them throughout the Roman Empire)[24] to a place called Durocobrivis, midway between Verulamium and Magiovinium. The mileage given puts this exactly on the site of Dunstable, at the junction of Watling Street and the Icknield Way, but for a long time doubts remained as to its existence. As recently as 1964 one author wrote that he had "spent several years searching for a Roman town at Dunstable without success and [was] forced to conclude that none existed".[25] However, the last twenty years have seen large-scale redevelopment in Dunstable town centre, and through rescue excavations by the Manshead Archaeological Society Roman occupation around the crossroads of Watling Street with the Icknield Way has been conclusively proved.

No substantial buildings have been found in Dunstable, although many pits and ditches have been uncovered in all four quadrants of the town. Because of the porous nature of the chalk, there was no surface water supply, and many wells were dug, some of them known to have been as much as 100 feet (30 metres) deep. To the south-west (Friary Field) a large cemetery has been excavated (see page 61);[26] in accordance with Roman law, this must have been situated outside the built-up area of the town.

Several factors probably combined to promote the growth of Durocobrivis. It has already been suggested (see page 18) that there was a military post of some sort, as it lay on an important road junction, and Watling Street was the supply line for the forces on the frontier to the north-west. It may have housed a garrison in the early years after the conquest, but even when peace was fully ensured, there was possibly a staging post for military and civilian personnel. The facilities may have included a stables to provide a change of horses, and possibly overnight accommodation as well. No such buildings have been located, although it is likely they were destroyed without record when the medieval town was built, or when cellars were dug beneath the buildings along the Watling Street frontage.

The presence of an official establishment, and the existence of a crossroads between two major long distance routes, would have quickly attracted those who hoped to make a living from the permanent residents and from passing traffic. Surrounding farms would find a market for their produce, and no doubt there would be those ready to act as middlemen and cream off a share of the profits. The income thereby gained would in turn attract suppliers of other specialised goods, such as pottery, tools and metalwork. The small, but growing, settlement would in this way become a market place and point of exchange for the surrounding countryside.

The settlement at Sandy may have developed in similar fashion, as the presence of members of the Catuvellaunian aristocracy in the Ivel valley perhaps prompted some sort of military presence in the early days after the conquest. Although identified by many antiquaries[27] as the "Salinae" mentioned in Ptolemy's *Geography* of the second century[28] mainly because of the similarity of the name, "Sandy" is in fact derived from *sand eg*, which is Old English for "sand island".[29] The name "Salinae" means "salt-works" and may indicate an otherwise unknown settlement on the North Sea coast, though it is much more likely to refer to Droitwich, Worcestershire, also known as "Salinae".[30]

As at Dunstable, no Roman buildings have been identified at Sandy, although there have been scattered finds of brick, stone and tile. However, the quality of the discoveries at Sandy over the last three centuries has been noticeably higher than at Dunstable, and the settlement, though small, was clearly not lacking in wealth.[31] The first finds were recorded in the 17th century, picked up by labourers on the market garden areas south-east of the modern town. Coins were gathered in large quantities, as well as small items of metalwork such as an intaglio (seal) ring, a bronze female head, and a mirror.[32] Many more Roman objects came to light with the construction of the Great Northern Railway (opened 1850), particularly during the extraction of gravel for ballast from a slight rise south-west of the town, known as Tower Hill.[33] Large numbers of complete pottery vessels, some containing ashes, revealed the existence of a cremation cemetery outside the town. Inhumations were also found, two of them in lead coffins. In more recent years, Roman material has been found in the municipal cemetery,[34] and elsewhere as a result of gravel quarrying.[35]

No plan of the settlement at Sandy has been recovered, and nothing is known of the layout of buildings. It perhaps had at its core an official establishment, either a military unit or administrative offices, and no doubt served as a market place for the surrounding countryside. It was probably the place of residence for wealthier members of the local society, anxious to display a Roman lifestyle by adopting "town" life.

Apart from Dunstable and Sandy, a few other settlements in Bedfordshire seem to be larger than the normal farmstead or villa. These are not towns, not even small ones, and perhaps the most useful term to apply to them is "village". Even this may be a little misleading, as they were more loosely arranged than a modern village — probably a series of occupation sites in close proximity to one another. At Limbury, north of Luton, where the line of the Icknield Way crosses the River Lea, gravel extraction and house building over the last 80 years have produced signs of occupation over a large area.[36]

Only a small part of that area has been studied by excavation, in which ditches, pits, hearths, cobbled floors and postholes have been recorded,[37] as well as some industrial activity.[38] Altogether, occupation evidence extends almost continuously alongside the Icknield Way for about half a mile north of the River Lea crossing. At the centre of the settlement there was possibly a villa, as there are reports which suggest that a mosaic pavement may have been discovered during building work in 1928.[39]

At Ruxox, near Flitwick (though in Maulden parish), a large area of Roman occupation has been discovered, initially by archaeological field survey.[40] In the 1950s, T.H. Gardner conducted a series of small trial excavations after identifying concentrations of Roman pottery in the ploughsoil. He demonstrated that an extensive Roman settlement existed alongside the now marshy areas of the Flit valley, and in some places Roman remains were actually uncovered beneath the later peat deposits.[41] Since then a series of investigations has been carried out by the Ampthill and District Archaeological Society, most recently recording features revealed during the construction of the Ampthill bypass. There

COPLE/WILLINGTON
Cropmarks

N

0   300m
1,000ft

18. Cropmarks between Cople and Willington, G278.

may have been a villa at the heart of the settlement, though many finds of a religious nature suggest that the focus was a temple (see page 56).

Another extensive settlement, lying between Cople and Willington, can be deduced from aerial photographs (fig. 18). Cropmarks indicate a series of enclosures extending alongside an old stream course, and regular ditches towards the western end were perhaps associated with a villa site. Roman material has been picked up from the surface, but nothing further is known.

Population

Attempting to calculate population for a period long before detailed documentary records is a very difficult exercise, and can never be much more than reasoned guesswork. Recent research has shown that there were many more settlements in Roman Britain than had previously been thought, and that the heavier soils were no longer covered by vast tracts of untouched forest. This has led to a reassessment of the low population figures which were once thought likely. A figure of five million for the whole of Roman Britain is probably a conservative estimate. In the immediately post-Roman period population declined. Despite another peak in the 13th century, it probably did not return to the maximum Roman level until about the 17th century. The countryside of Roman Britain therefore resembled the settled landscape of Stuart England much more than the traditionally accepted picture of isolated settlements in an empty wilderness.

Chapter 5

TRADE AND ECONOMY

The inhabitants of Roman Bedfordshire were bound together by political, administrative, and probably tenurial, rights and obligations. In addition to these social relationships, and to a large extent overlapping with them, was a wide network of economic interconnections. A rural settlement in Roman Britain, especially in the lowland area, was by no means self-sufficient. Agriculture provided much of the food for the farmstead or villa which produced it, but most of the household goods, the personal possessions, and the agricultural implements, had to be acquired from elsewhere. The complexity of the commercial and economic life of the province can be demonstrated by looking at the surviving material possessions which might be encountered on a Roman site, from the building itself to the jewellery worn by the occupants, and by considering how those possessions were obtained.

Agriculture and its products

Farmsteads and villas were engaged in mixed agriculture, both arable and stock farming. Grain (particularly wheat and barley) was probably the most financially rewarding of crops. Although a certain amount would be taken by the authorities in the form of tax for army supplies, this may have brought as much benefit in the long term, through stimulating production, as it did hardship in the short term. Grain for sale was dried to prevent germination, and this was one of the uses of the drying ovens which were a common feature of rural sites. Examples are known from Odell (fig. 19), Bromham[1] and Flitwick.[2] They probably served for many processes which required a steady heat, including the malting of barley for home-brewed ale.

As with most agricultural produce, the immediate outlet for grain was the near-

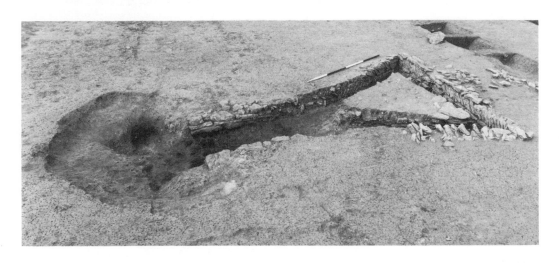

19. Drying oven, Odell, G187.

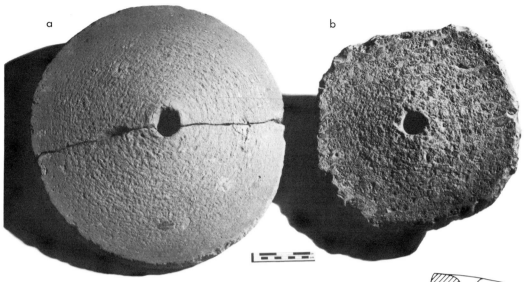

20. *Rotary querns: (a) lower stone of millstone grit, Sandy, G217; (b) lower stone of Hertfordshire conglomerate, Bedford, G22; (c) reconstruction.*

est market where it may have been ground for sale as flour, or sold to bakers whose shops served passing traffic or market visitors. "A quantity of charred wheat . . amounting to near thirty quarters [840 lb or 380 kg]" found at Sandy during the extraction of gravel for railway ballast[3] may have been part of the stock of a corn merchant in the town, perhaps charred by an accident in drying, or by a store-room fire.

Grain kept for home consumption was ground on rotary millstones, or "beehive" querns (fig. 20). The nearest available stone for Bedfordshire querns was Hertfordshire conglomerate, or puddingstone. Millstone grit from the Pennines increased in popularity as the development of distribution networks made it easier to obtain. The upper end of the market was supplied during the earlier Roman period by Andernach lava from the Rhineland; querns of this material have been found only in and near Dunstable, where there was probably a retail outlet.[4] Because transport costs were so high, querns may usually have been shipped in a finished state. One quern found at Caddington,[5] however, is a roughed-out example in Hertfordshire conglomerate, which it was presumably intended to finish when it reached its destination. Watermills were known in Roman Britain, where grain was ground on a large-scale commercial basis; none has been positively identified in Bedfordshire, but there may have been some on the major water-courses.

Apart from grain, farms provided vegetables for local consumption, but since these are more perishable than grain, they are less easily recoverable. Cherrystones and hazelnut shells found in the bottom of a well in Dunstable had probably been gathered from the wild.[6]

The most common farm animals, known only from their skeletal remains, seem to have been cattle, and sheep or goats. The latter have identical skeletons and can only be distinguished by their horn cores; both sheep and goat horns have been found, but goats were much less numerous than sheep. Pigs were also kept for meat. As with the crops, some of the animal produce would have been retained for home processing, and the surplus disposed of through the market place. Dairy products were consumed, from cattle, sheep and goats, and pottery vessels with perforated bases may have been used as cheese presses.

Sheep's wool provided the commonest source of material for clothing, and some was spun and woven at home. Spindle-whorls were made out of anything that was available, such as pottery (including fragments of broken vessels), chalk or bone; a bone spindlewhorl from Limbury (fig. 21) was turned on a lathe. Triangular weights provide the only material remains of upright domestic looms (fig. 22). Linen was also known, though it was less common than wool. A fragment of textile (probably linen) has been found in Dunstable, preserved in the corrosion of a bronze coin;[7] it may have come from the purse in which the coin was kept. Apart from that made on a domestic scale, specialist merchants traded in cloth, especially the finer quality products. As part of the production of woollen clothing, the material went through the fulling process, which used fuller's earth and stale urine to remove the natural fats from the cloth. There is

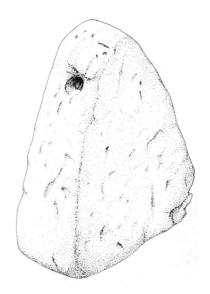

22. *Clay loomweight, Kensworth Common (Whipsnade parish, G277). Scale 2:3.*

a tradition that the Romans quarried fuller's earth from the Aspley Heath area,[8] though there is no evidence to confirm this.

Meat products also supplied both home consumption and the local market. In some towns of Roman Britain, animal bone debris has enabled butcher's shops to be identified, and these probably existed in any centre of population to provide meat for the inhabitants not engaged in agriculture. Leather served many functions, although few leather goods survive. Leather footwear has been found in waterlogged conditions at Biddenham (see fig. 56), Dunstable (fig. 23) and Ruxox.[9]

While simple shoes or sandals may have been made at home, hard-wearing working boots with hobnails in the soles were a specialist product. Some villas probably had facilities for tanning leather for the wholesale trade. A cobbler's last found at Sandy[10] is likely to have belonged to a professional shoe-maker. Animal horn was not wasted: a group of cattle, sheep and goat horn cores, found

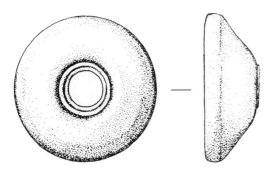

21. *Bone spindlewhorl, Limbury, G154. Scale 1:1.*

23. Insole from a leather shoe, from a well at Dunstable, G63. Scale 1:2.

in the modern cemetery at Sandy,[11] may have been the waste products from a horn workshop, though it is not known what the workshop was producing. Bone provided the raw material for a wide range of domestic items, such as decorated dress pins, needles, and knife handles, most of these again available through specialist workshops (fig. 24).

Some sites have produced the remains of red, roe and fallow deer.[12] Where only antlers are found, these may have been collected after they had been shed. Other bones suggest that deer were occasionally hunted. Hunting was a popular pursuit in Roman Britain, and hunting scenes are a common decorative feature on some of the finer pottery (fig. 25). Dogs were used in the chase and for herding stock.

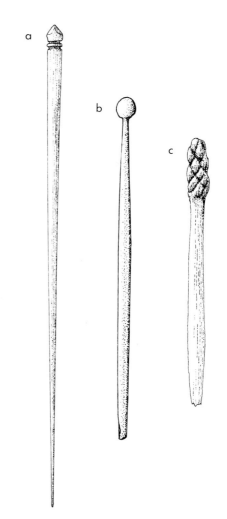

24. Bone pins: (a), (b) Tempsford, G246; (c) Ruxox, G174. Scale 1:1.

25. Fragment of colour-coated beaker, Putnoe (G17), showing hunt scene. Scale 1:2.

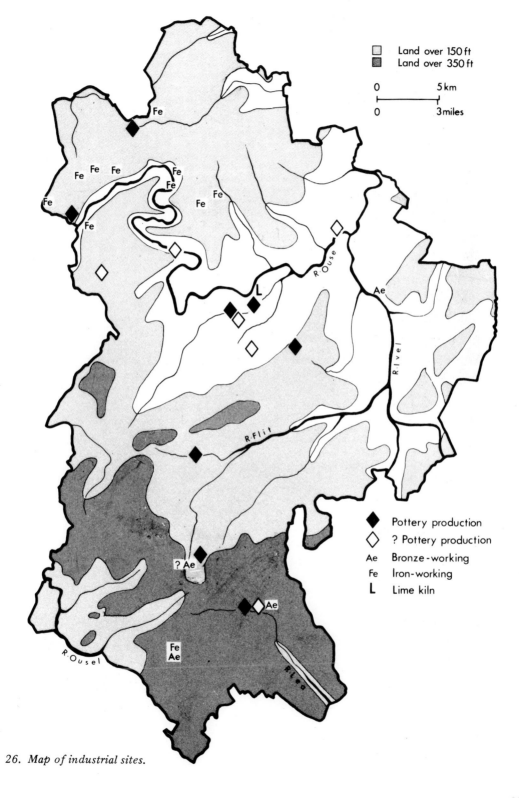

Land over 150 ft
Land over 350 ft

0   5 km
0   3 miles

Fe

Fe Fe Fe   Fe
                Fe
Fe   Fe
    Fe   Fe Fe

R. Ouse

Ae

R i v e l

L

Ae

R. Flit

? Ae

Ae

Fe
Ae

R. Ousel

R. Lea

◆ Pottery production
◇ ? Pottery production
Ae Bronze-working
Fe Iron-working
L   Lime kiln

26. Map of industrial sites.

The discovery of chicken bones at Odell, Dunstable,[13] Luton[14] and Tottern-hoe[15] suggests that chicken was bred for the table. Fowl may have been more popular than skeletal remains suggest, as bird bones tend to survive less well than those of the larger animals.

Another favourite food was shellfish: trade in oysters was well-developed in the Roman world, in spite of the apparent risks of contamination. Many sites in the county, especially more wealthy settlements, have produced oyster shells,[16] while whelks and scallops have been found in Dunstable.[17]

Surplus produce secured an income with which the rural population could obtain goods produced by specialist industries and craftsmen (see fig.26). Trade and commerce was based on coinage, and the economy was complex enough to support middle-men between the producer and his customer. A certain proportion of the population, over and above the officers of the military and civilian administration, were therefore not directly involved in production. Merchants no doubt entered Britain from the continent, continuing the pre-Roman commercial links, but opportunist natives also took their own share of the commerce. In towns such as Verulamium, there is evidence, in the layout of streets and shops, of planned development schemes, each probably set up by one man with sufficient land and capital; the various premises were then let out to craftsmen and retailers. Although this may have been the case at Dunstable and Sandy, it cannot be confirmed because of the lack of evidence. Similarly at Limbury,[18] where there was an extended area of settlement which probably included some industrial premises,[19] a native owner may have used his wealth and control over land to encourage the development of commercial enterprise, from which he reaped the benefit.

Pottery: Kitchen and Table

The most common artefact to be recovered from Roman sites is pottery, varying in quality (as in price) from coarse kitchen vessels to fine tableware. The finer the pottery, the further it was likely to travel from its place of production, but many of the coarseware vessels found in Bedfordshire were made in or

27. *Pottery vessels in calcite-tempered fabric: (a) cooking pot, Bedfordshire, exact provenance uncertain; (b) fragment of storage jar, Bromham, G36.*

28. Grey ware vessels: (a), (b), (d) Sandy, probably G211; (c) Kempston, G125.

near the county. Several centres of pottery production are known. At Lodge Farm, Harrold, some kilns were discovered in 1968,[20] and a series of excavations has shown that cooking pots and storage jars were made here throughout the Roman period, from local clays tempered with crushed shelly limestone. The unusually high number of coins from the site is an indication of the commercial nature of the pottery production, although other finds, such as items of jewellery and a spindlewhorl, suggest that there was domestic occupation as well as commercial activity. As a centre for pottery production it was ideally sited. There was clay for the main body of the pots, and limestone which could be crushed to provide tempering (calcite); stone was also used as a building material for the kilns. A steady supply of fuel was probably obtained, by careful management, from woodland on the clay ridge to the north-west. The river valley was an easy line of communication to local consumers, and its good quality land would provide for small-scale agricultural production at those times of year when the manufacture of pottery did not require the attention of all the occupants.

Calcite- or shell-tempered pottery (fig. 27) has been found throughout Bedfordshire, though it does seem to constitute a higher percentage of the pottery used in the north of the county, mainly because it was nearer the main source of supply. But it is unlikely that all such pottery originated from Harrold. Other kilns probably existed along the Ouse valley; the report of kiln bars and "wasters" (the broken fragments of badly fired vessels) from the settlement excavated at Bromham[21] may indicate another production site.

Another common pottery fabric was sand-tempered "grey ware", which served as the tableware in daily use for many Roman households. The forms available included bowls and jars, dishes and beakers (fig. 28). Grey ware was produced at a series of sites to the south-east of Bedford, notably at Mile Road,[22] though other kilns have been identified in Eastcotts[23] and Cardington[24] parishes. The fabric was harder than the shelly wares, being tempered with sand. It was usually a light or dark shade of grey, although red pottery could be produced if oxygen entered the kiln during firing. As at Harrold, excavations at Mile Road have uncovered traces of domestic occupation as well as industrial activity. Grey ware is found on most Roman sites, and there are probably other centres of production in the county awaiting discovery. There is evidence that the purchasers of such pottery did not necessarily make use of the nearest manufacturing site. At the villa at Newnham, for example, only a mile or so from the Mile Road kilns, though on the other side of the Ouse, quantities of grey ware have been found, but the exact composition of the fabrics does not seem to match those produced at Mile Road.[25] The implication of this is that pottery manufacturers did not necessarily sell directly to nearby settlements, but presumably sent their products to a market centre for the retail trade.

Elsewhere in the county, the existence of potteries is suggested by the discovery of kiln remains, or of wasters, although the type of pottery produced has not been recorded. An isolated knoll called Foxburrow,[26] in Toddington parish (now the site of the Toddington service station on the M1), was cut into by Major Cooper Cooper of Toddington Manor and James Wyatt in 1874, after pottery fragments had been thrown up when some agricultural drains were being dug. The "numerous fragments of small urns, slightly baked . . . . a large quantity of ashes and charred wood, with stones and boulders discoloured by fire"[27] sound very like the debris which would be encountered on a pottery manufacturing site, and a later reference to clay bars "like furnace bars"[28] seems to describe the fire-bars on which vessels would be stood at the base of a pottery kiln. Similar clay bars, found with potsherds and baked clay, south of Waulud's Bank, Luton in 1882, were probably also from a pottery kiln.[29] Not far away, in excavations on the extensive settlement at Limbury during housing development in 1953, a quantity of crushed grit was

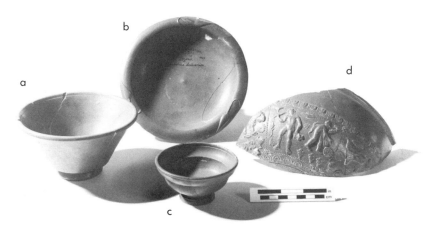

29. *Samian vessels: (a) Greenfield, G96; (b), (c) Kempston, G125; (d) Sandy, G212.*

40

found. It has been suggested this may have been intended for the manufacture of mortaria, pottery bowls with grit embedded into the inside face, used as vegetable mixing bowls.[30] At Tempsford, pottery wasters were found in pits filled with soot and ash, in an area which probably lay close to a Roman villa;[31] jars with manufacturing blemishes found with cremations at Sandy[32] and Roxton[33] may have been purchased as seconds from kilns not far away.

Long-distance trade in fine tableware was already known in the days before the Roman invasion. The cremation burials of the Belgic aristocracy were frequently accompanied by vessels of the glossy red "samian" ware from Gaul. The large number of samian vessels found with the Stanfordbury burials[34] was probably imported during the decade before the conquest (see page 15). The trade increased in volume throughout the 1st century, with consignments being shipped from production centres in South Gaul. In the 2nd century, potteries in central and eastern Gaul took over the business, and continued to send vessels to Britain until the middle of the 3rd century, although in reduced quantity after c. AD 200. Few settlements would have been without a certain amount of samian tableware (fig. 29), although the higher the social status the greater the quantity. The value of samian as a personal possession is indicated by the examples which were repaired with lead rivets (fig. 30). Samian vessels were frequently stamped with the name of the potter (fig. 31).

The samian potteries did not enjoy a monopoly on the supply of fine wares, and gradually production centres in Britain, perhaps initially set up by immigrant craftsmen, took an increasing share of the market. Most notable in the east Midlands area were the kilns in the Nene

30. Samian dish repaired with lead rivets, Sandy, probably G211. Scale 1:4.

valley, near Peterborough. These produced "colour-coated" pottery, often called "Castor ware", which was light in colour but covered with a thin slip of darker clay, to give an orange or brown, olive or black coat. Further decoration might be applied, in the form of a trailed white slip, with abstract designs of vegetation, or hunting scenes with dogs and hares (see figs. 1 and 25). Much of the colour-coated pottery found in Bedfordshire probably came from the Nene valley, but some originated in Oxfordshire and the New Forest, and some from even as far as the German Rhineland.

Before and during the Roman period, amphorae were imported into Britain from the continent, not for their own sake, but because of their contents. They

31. Potter's stamp (GIPPI. M) on samian cup from Greenfield (see fig. 29a). Scale 2:1.

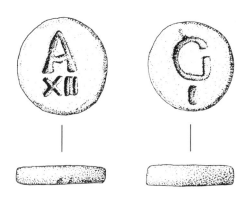

32. Clay gaming counters, Kempston, G125. Scale 1:1.

were usually shipped from southern Spain, and contained wine, oil or fish sauce. No doubt they were re-used as storage vessels when emptied of their original contents (see fig. 2).

Smaller artefacts could also be made of fired clay. Two gaming counters, found in a Roman cemetery at Kempston (fig. 32), were made for use with some sort of board game.

Metalwork

Bedfordshire has no deposits of metal ores, and all metal objects — tools, utensils, ornaments — had to be brought in from elsewhere, either as the raw materials, or as the finished product. All minerals in the Roman Empire were technically state-owned, but many mining and quarrying operations were leased out to private enterprise. There were many workshops and craftsmen — gold and silversmiths, jewellers working in copper and bronze, blacksmiths and farriers.

Gold from the imperial mines at Dolaucothi, near Llandovery in Dyfed, and silver extracted from the lead ores of the Mendips and Derbyshire, went mainly into the imperial treasury to be minted as coins. However, a certain amount found its way into the jewellery trade, and a goldsmith's workshop is known to have existed at Verulamium.[35] A silver finger-ring has been found at Dunstable (with a small bronze key mounted on it)[36] and another at Sandy.[37]

A gold ring which came to light at Biddenham (fig. 33) is of a very rare type, and may have been a specially commissioned item.

Bronze was used for a wide range of objects, from jewellery and small utensils to large vessels. Copper was mined in north Wales, although tin seems to have been mostly imported from north Spain, as the Cornish mines were not seriously exploited until towards the end of the Roman occupation. A bronzesmith would probably acquire the copper and tin in their raw state, and melt them together in a crucible to create the alloy, which he would then pour into a stone or pot-

33. Peripheral photograph of gold ring, Biddenham (G27), showing lettering. Scale 2:1. Diameter of ring 20 mm/0.8 inches. (Copyright British Museum)

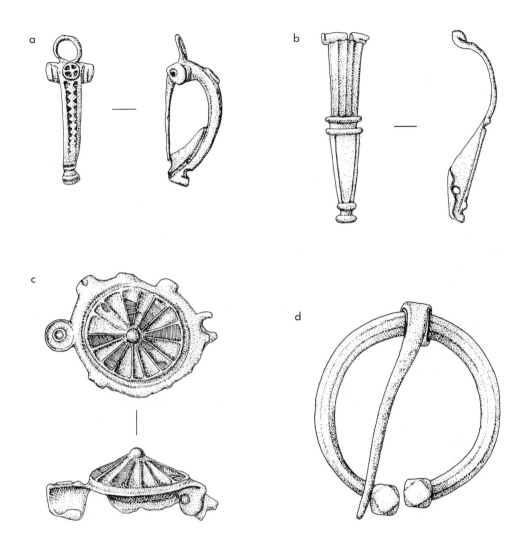

34. *Bronze brooches: (a) Dunstable, G76; (b) Sandy, probably G211; (c) with enamel inlay, Bedfordshire, exact provenance uncertain; (d) Apsley End, Shillington, G229. Scale 1:1.*

tery mould. A bronzesmith may have worked in the Limbury area, as a smelting furnace and crucible have been found there,[38] and a bronzesmith's hearth has been reported from Dunstable.[39] It has been suggested that fragments of bronze from Sandy were off-cuts from the manufacture of small bronze objects on the site.[40] At Fancott, near Toddington, "lumps of nearly pure copper, mixed with wood charcoal, bones, ashes, etc"

were found in the early 19th century, from an area where some Roman pottery was also discovered.[41] This activity cannot be said to be definitely Roman in date, but it may mark another bronze workshop. Even the debris from bronze-working was utilised: an oculist's stamp from Harrold (see page 54 and fig. 53) refers to ointments made from copper ore and the waste flakes from copper-working.[42]

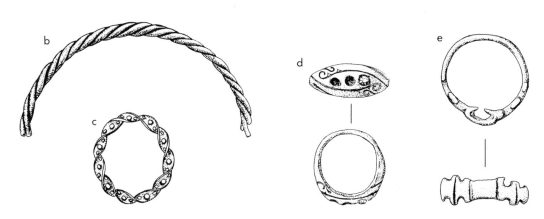

35. Bronze bracelets and rings: (a), (b) Newnham, G13; (c), (d) Ruxox, G174; (e) Kempston, G125. Scale 1:1.

The most common bronze ornaments were brooches, used as garment fasteners throughout the Roman period (fig. 34). These were frequently bow brooches (the forerunner of the safety-pin), but also might be of penannular form, or fashioned out of small circular plates. Fine examples could be inlaid with an enamel decoration, in red, blue, white or green. Bracelets (fig. 35a, b) could be either of flat bronze strips, sometimes decorated with incised lines, or of twisted bronze wire. Finger-rings were occasionally elaborately decorated (fig. 35c-e) or might incorporate gemstones, engraved for use as a seal (see figs. 55 and 60). Pins, used as dress fastenings, often had decorated heads (fig. 36a); some bronze needles have been found, although they were also made of bone. Toilet implements were a common personal item, and included tweezers, nail-cleaners and earscoops, often forming a set attached to a bronze ring (fig. 36b), while small spatulas were used for extracting oint-

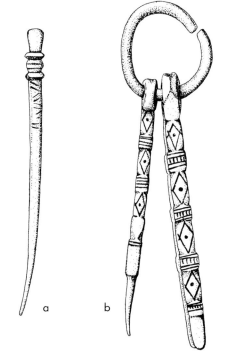

36. (a) Bronze pin, Puddlehill, G119; (b) bronze toilet set, incorporating tweezers and nail-cleaner, Maiden Bower, Houghton Regis, G120. Scale 1:1.

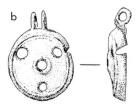 

37. (a) Iron stylus, Limbury, G154; (b) bronze seal box lid, Newnham, G13; (c) bronze casket handle, Newnham. Scale 1:1.

ments or cosmetics from small bottles (see fig. 49b).

As literacy increased so did the use of the stylus, made of bronze or iron (fig. 37a), which had a point at one end for writing on a wax tablet, and was flattened at the other for use as an eraser; a wooden fragment from a tablet was found at Odell.[43] If a tablet was sent as a letter, the two halves of the wooden case would be folded together, and the string ties sealed, using a personal seal box to apply the stamp (fig. 37b). Some household containers, perhaps jewellery boxes or small cupboards, were occasionally furnished with handles (fig. 37c) and bronze locks.

Several small bronze figurines have been found in the county, though none can now be traced. They include a soldier from Podington,[44] and a "slave" from Kempston.[45] Bronze heads from Bromham[46] and Sandy[47] seem to have been steelyard weights, perhaps used by their owners in commercial transactions, to

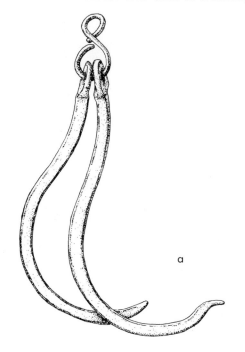

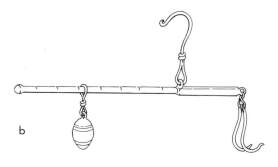

38. (a) Bronze hooks, Newnham, scale 1:1; (b) reconstruction of steelyard, showing use of hooks and steelyard weight.

39. Bronze bowls, Sandy, G215.

check the weight of grain or other goods. A pair of bronze hooks from Newnham probably also came from a weighing device (fig. 38).

Some of the bronze objects found in Bedfordshire display a high level of skilled craftsmanship, and were probably imported from continental workshops. A group of late Roman bowls was uncovered at Sandy when the railway branch line was constructed to Potton in 1856 (fig. 39). From two separate sites in Biggles-

40. Bronze patera with decorated handle, Biggleswade, G28. Length 325 mm/12.9 inches. (Copyright Cambridge University Museum of Archaeology and Anthropology).

41. Bronze lamp, Biggleswade, G29. Scale 1:2.

worker's stock of raw material.[51] Lead was also one of the metals used in producing pewter, the other being tin. Pewter vessels were produced for use as tableware towards the end of the Roman period (fig. 43).

Of all the metals in use in Roman Bedfordshire, iron was the nearest to hand. While large-scale operations were concentrated in the Weald of Kent and the Forest of Dean, initially under imperial control, the ironstones of Northamptonshire were also exploited, probably by private concerns. Concentrations of smelting slag are very common in Northamptonshire, and extend into the northwest corner of Bedfordshire.[52] These are often undated, but sufficient numbers have been found in association with Roman pottery to show that iron smelting was being carried out in the county

wade, both of them probably burials, have come a 1st century patera with a ram's head handle (fig. 40) and a bronze lamp (fig. 41). A mount from Hyde parish is decorated with the popular hunt scene of a hound and stag, but the function of the object is uncertain (fig. 42).

Objects of lead are rarely found, and when the metal does occur it is usually in the form of unrecognisable fragments, perhaps as the waste from small repair jobs, such as the mending of pottery vessels referred to above. The main use that has been identified in Bedfordshire is for lead coffins, which have been found at Dunstable[48] and Clapham,[49] with two being uncovered in Sandy.[50] All these were discovered during the 19th century, and none has survived. Such bulky and heavy items are unlikely to have been transported in their finished state, and were probably made up in workshops close to their eventual resting-place. A lead ingot, or pig, said to have been found at Sandy, was probably part of a lead-

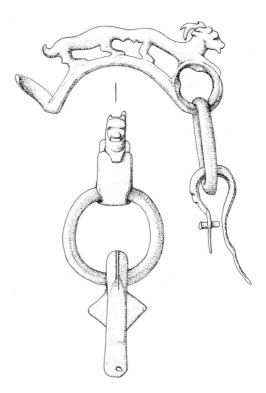

42. Bronze mount, Hyde, G124. Scale 2:3.

43. Pewter dish (restored), Putnoe, G17. Scale 1:3.

during the Roman period.

The smelting process required large amounts of fuel, and it was clearly considered economic to transport the iron ore to the fuel supply, provided by charcoal from the woodland which survived on the boulder clay uplands of north Bedfordshire. There were, however, no vast tracts of undisturbed tree cover — the number of Roman sites in the area shows that much woodland had been cleared — and the iron smelters probably managed their fuel supply by regular coppicing of the remaining woodland, rather than by indiscriminate felling. Iron ore was smelted in small furnaces, driving off impurities as slag, and resulting in a bloom which could be further improved by hammering out the impurities using a smithing furnace. It seems that smelting was carried out as a side-line at some of the more important sites in north Bedfordshire: at a villa in Bletsoe parish, molten ironstone fragments were found along with some charcoal;[53] at Radwell,

a flue or stokehole filled with black slag was probably part of a furnace.[54]

Iron was used for all heavy-duty tools and implements, for those which required a sharp and durable cutting edge, and for many other purposes in home and workshop. Ploughs, built with a wooden frame, had an iron-tipped share; they were improved by the introduction of a vertically mounted coulter to cut through the earth (fig. 44). The plough teams were urged on with ox-goads, of which an example has been reported from Dunstable.[55] A harvesting sickle has been found at Ruxox,[56] and a mower would often carry his own portable anvil,[57] for hammering out nicks in the blade. The edge would then be restored using a small hone or whetstone, usually made from millstone grit (fig. 45). A rake from Dunstable[58] may have been used in haymaking. In the field of transport, cart fittings, including hub bands, lynch pins and an axle box, have been found in a hoard of ironwork at Sandy.[59] Part of a farrier's equipment has been preserved in a three-legged buttress, used for steadying a horse's foot during shoeing, also from Sandy.[60] Linked iron bars found at Limbury (fig. 46a) may be the remains of a horse bit.

An iron barrel lock from Tempsford (fig. 46b) was probably used to secure a substantial door. From the same site, a gouge (fig. 47c) may have been part of a carpenter's tool kit. Knives were very common implements, both at home and at work (fig. 47a). From a well at Dunstable came the iron hoops of a bucket (and the wooden staves which they se-

44. Plough coulter, Sandy, G217. Length 840 mm/33 inches.

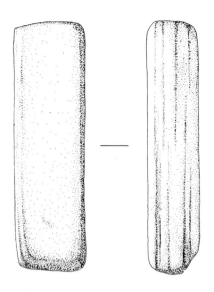

45. Whetstone, Newnham, G13. Scale 1:1.

cured), as well as a grapple which may have been lost in trying to retrieve it.[61]

Weapons are not very common, as carrying them was forbidden to civilians. Several arrowheads have, however, been found in Dunstable[62] and spearheads are known from Tempsford (fig. 47b) and Harrold.[63] A sword, said to have been discovered along with the three bronze bowls from Sandy, had an interesting end: Sir William Peel, who promoted the construction of the Sandy-Potton railway line, during which it was found, "being a *fighting man*, had one made from it for his own use, which he used in India during the mutiny, where he fell at Lucknow".[64]

From the wide range of uses for ironwork, it is clear that a blacksmith would have been a very valuable member of the Roman community, both for the provision of new tools and for the repair

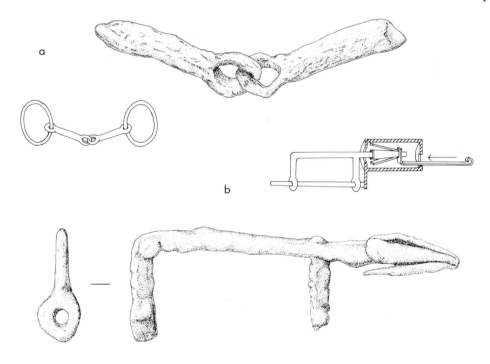

46. (a) Linked iron bars, Limbury (G154), showing possible reconstruction as a horse bit; (b) barrel lock bolt, Tempsford (G246), with reconstruction to show function. Object scales 2:3.

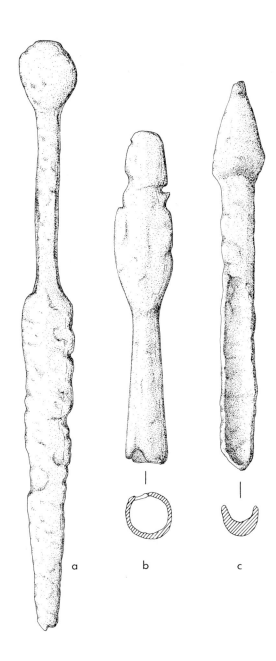

48. *Glass jug, Shefford, G223. Height 195 mm/ 7.7 inches. (Copyright Cambridge University Museum of Archaeology and Anthropology).*

of old ones. No doubt each of the larger settlements in the county had one or more smithies, obtaining their raw materials from the smelting sites in the north-west, with perhaps some in Sandy and Dunstable specialising in farrier's work for through traffic. An itinerant service may also have been provided to rural settlements, to deal with heavy implements and construction work, and most villas and farmsteads probably had their own forge.

Glass and Jet

Another material available to the population of Roman Britain was glass. Its main use was in high quality tableware — jugs, bottles and bowls — but window glass was also known, and probably quite

47. *(a) Iron knife or dagger blade, Ruxox, G174; (b) iron spearhead, (c) iron gouge, Tempsford, G246. Scale 2:3.*

common on wealthier sites. Most of the glassware was imported, continuing the trade in items such as those buried at Stanfordbury.[65] Many of the better examples which have survived are of 1st century date, including a jug from Shefford (fig. 48) and an ointment bottle from Northill (fig. 49a). A 3rd century flagon neck, found in the modern cemetery at Sandy, is thought to have come from the Cologne area of the Rhine Valley, where glass manufacture was a thriving industry (fig. 50).[66] British glass vessels were of much poorer quality, and not common. Fragments of window glass found at Radwell [67] were probably made in Britain, but it is not known where. Glass beads were a common ornament, and many were found in necklaces in the Dunstable cemetery.[68]

Kimmeridge shale from Dorset, and Whitby jet from north Yorkshire, came to the Bedfordshire area in the form of ornaments. Shale was used in the late Iron Age, even for such large items as two lathe-turned vases from the cremation burial at Old Warden (see page 15),[69]

50. *Glass flagon neck, Sandy, G212. Scale 2:3.*

a   b

49. (a) *Glass ointment bottle, Northill, G181;*
(b) *bronze ligula, Odell, G187. Scale 1:2*

although the bracelet and gaming counters from Stanfordbury were a more normal use. The best collection of jet ornaments has again come from the Dunstable cemetery, where a bracelet, a pin with a faceted head, and beads were buried as grave-offerings.[70]

Buildings

Iron Age building techniques in the Bedfordshire area revolved around the use of timber. Stone buildings were unknown, and even the highest quality structures had timber frames, infilled with wattle and daub, and roofed with thatch. With the development of a Roman way of life, stone became more fashionable, especially in the homes of the upper classes, though even then it was used mainly for the lower courses of walls, with timber-work above them. The type of stone employed tended to be that available locally. Limestone was common in north Bedfordshire, and could be used as rubble for foundations or the core of walls, but could also be dressed with architectural details for faces and corners. Dressed stone may occur in the surface scatter above villa sites, as at Carlton[71] and Odell.[72] Across the centre of the county, coinciding with the greensand ridge, sandstone is found. Squared sandstone blocks have been picked up at Sandy;[73] the drying oven at Flitwick was built on a sandstone footing;[74] a well, probably Roman, found in Leighton Buzzard, was lined with the same material.[75] Further south, a very hard form of chalk known as clunch turns up in the villa at Totternhoe,[76] and it is almost certain that the Totternhoe clunch quarries, so productive in medieval and later times, were first worked during the Roman period. The builders of the Totternhoe villa also made use of local flint.

Many of the villa sites probably had their own quarries which were worked as and when necessary. There are some signs however of imported stone for special purposes. From the villa at Tempsford,[77] for example, came some fragments of marble which had probably formed decorative wall-facings. The marble was almost certainly continental in origin, and supplied by a specialist builder.

The use of stone, and the development of other features of Roman buildings, such as hypocausts and tessellated or mosaic floors, required the production of a good quality mortar. The main ingredient of this was lime, produced by burning limestone or chalk, which was probably done on the building site itself. A lime kiln of 2nd century date has been discovered at Mill Farm, east of Bedford,[78] where the construction of a major sewage pipe in 1977 revealed a curved limestone footing, lined with clay,

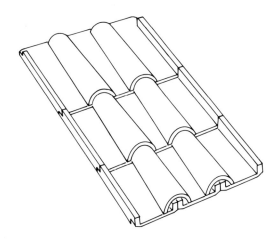

51. *Section of tiled roof.*

which had been subjected to high temperatures. Layers of charcoal and lime enabled its function to be identified. With the addition of sand and crushed brick or tile, a very hard mortar could be produced, known as *opus signinum*. It is quite possible that a "bed of concrete" found beneath some Saxon burials at Toddington in 1883, was a Roman floor of this material.[79]

Tiles were used for a variety of building purposes. Roofing tiles came in two forms, the *tegula*, which was a flat tile with side flanges, and the *imbrex*, a half cylinder shape which fitted over adjacent *tegulae* to give a water-tight covering (fig. 51). Flue tiles were set into those buildings which had hypocaust heating systems; wedge-shaped tiles, or voussoirs, formed the arches of the channels through which hot air was directed from the furnace area beneath the floor; box tiles were used to create vertical flues within the walls, to spread the heat and allow the escape of hot air and fumes (fig. 52). These box tiles can easily be distinguished, even from small fragments, because their outer sides were scored while the clay was still wet, to allow them to be keyed into the mortar. Brick-tiles were used for a number of purposes. They were sometimes introduced as string courses into stone walls to give extra strength (this can still be seen in the Roman town walls at Verulamium). Stacked in piles, or *pilae,* they formed supports for raised floors beneath which hot air could be circulated. Larger flat square tiles capped the *pilae* and over this base further tiles and mortar could be added, with mosaic tesserae if required (see fig. 15).

Tiles came in varying qualities. At the villa at Newnham[80] were found tiles in both a calcite-tempered and a hard red sandy fabric. Probably the latter was used for the main living quarters and the former for buildings of less social importance. Calcite tiles of all types were made at the pottery kilns at Harrold,[81] but no production site has been found for the sandy tiles. Occasionally limestone roof slates are found, as at the villa at Bletsoe.[82]

In spite of the increased use of stone in building, timber remained an important material. Most farmsteads had only timber buildings, and many of the agricultural buildings on villa sites were built without stone. Some structures probably had a mixture of the two, with a timber frame resting on stone foundations. Timber for the main structural beams, and smaller wood for wattle infill, was probably available in most localities. The use of wattle and daub has been reported from several sites,[83] usually identified from the fragments of daub, with wattle impressions in them. Many buildings would still have been thatched rather than tiled.

Much building construction was probably on a do-it-yourself basis, especially on rural farmsteads, or when agricultural sheds were required on villa estates.

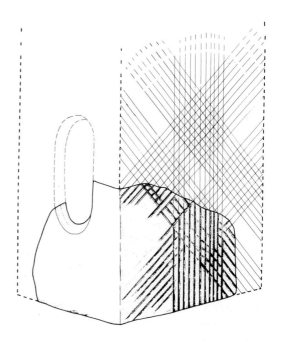

52. *Box flue tile (reconstructed), Newnham.*

However, building at the upper end of the market was undertaken by specialist businesses. This would certainly be the case when interior decoration — mosaics and wall-painting — were involved. The earliest craftsmen came over from the continent until British-based businesses developed. These were located in the towns, where Roman building techniques were first adopted, and were patronised by country residences in the surrounding areas. Where mosaics have been recorded in Bedfordshire, as at Totternhoe (see fig. 13), these may have been commissioned from a firm based at Verulamium. Unfortunately, the preservation of mosaics in the county is so poor that it is not possible to examine them artistically, and assess the origin of their designs. The only description of that reported from Limbury is of "a lovely floor, with a

G·IVN·TERTVLLI·DIA
LEPID·AD·ASPR·ET·C

G·IVN·TERTVLI
DIAMISVSAD·CIC

53. Oculist's stamp, Harrold (G104), and the stamped inscriptions.

head in the centre of a different colour."[84] Most of the mosaics reported are known only from scattered finds of tesserae. Similarly the incidence of painted wall plaster is so slight as to provide little useful information about styles in the county.

Three Oculists

The craftsmen, tradesmen, merchants and shopkeepers working in the Bedfordshire area in Roman times are almost without exception anonymous. The few names which are known have survived on the stamps with which the suppliers of eye ointments marked their products. An example from Sandy[85] mentions Gaius Valerius Amandus and Gaius Valerius Valentinus, who were probably either brothers or father and son, and whose tripartite names show that they were Roman citizens.

Another stamp from Harrold (fig. 53), almost certainly from the site of the pottery kilns at Lodge Farm, belonged to Gaius Junius Tertullus.[86] The inscriptions in full read "G(aii) Iun(ii) Tertulli dialepidos ad aspritudines et c(icatrices)" and "G(aii) Iun(ii) Tertulli diamisus ad cic (atrices)". They refer to an ointment made from the waste flakes from copperworking, for roughness and scars, and one prepared from copper pyrites, also for scars. The use of such preparations was common in the classical world,[87] and it seems that this particular oculist had a business arrangement with a copper workshop.

Chapter 6

RELIGION

Many of the features of life in Roman Britain were a fusion of Iron Age and Roman practices. This was particularly true of religious beliefs. Classical religions recognised many deities who were to be placated and respected and the Roman religious outlook had no difficulty in accepting the gods and goddesses of conquered peoples. Similarly, Celtic beliefs offered no barrier to the absorption of members of the Roman pantheon. The result was often the identification of the new Roman gods with the native deities. Some resistance was encountered at first to the introduction of the imperial cult, whereby deceased emperors, and, by

association, the spirits of living emperors, were deified and worshipped; during the Boudican episode, for example, the temple of Claudius in Camulodunum was destroyed. But even this opposition did not last, and native nobles were expected to serve their time on the provincial council which was responsible for the ceremonies connected with the cult. Temples of classical type seem to have been located mainly in the larger towns, but other religious sites, born out of the fusion of classical and native beliefs, were probably common in other settlements and in the countryside, and most houses would have been served by a

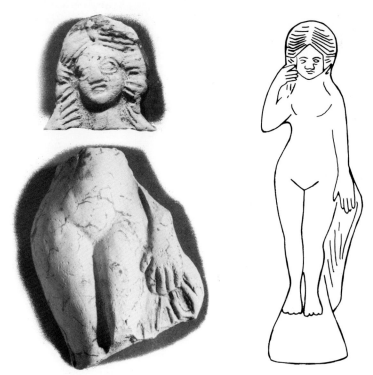

54. *Fragments of pipeclay figurines, Ruxox (G174; scale 1:1), with a reconstruction drawing.*

domestic shrine.

Sacred sites

The existence of temples or shrines can be deduced from objects of a religious nature found in several places in the county. There was almost certainly an important sacred site at Ruxox, where many fragments of small figurines and several gemstones (intaglios) have been brought to the surface by the plough. The figurines (fig. 54) show the goddess Venus; they are made of pipe-clay and are of a type which was mass-produced in Gaul specifically for use as ritual offerings. Intaglios were seal rings, usually engraved with representations of gods or goddesses, or heroes of the classical world. The designs chosen were particularly relevant to the character or occupation of the owner. Their popularity as votive objects probably arose from this close association with the personality of the donor. An example from Ruxox (fig. 55), of paste with small fragments of the iron ring remaining, shows Bacchus reclining, with small Cupid figures in front of him. Minerva stands to the side, holding a little figure of victory and a spear, with a shield at her feet.[1]

55. Intaglio stone, Ruxox. Scale 4:1.

A stone-lined well found at Biddenham in 1857 contained fragments of sculpture, including parts of a human figure (fig. 56). These may have decorated a shrine, although the hollowed stone slab interpreted as an altar for libation was probably the basal stone for a door jamb. A portable stone altar has been found in the Roman cemetery at Kempston (fig. 57).

Representations of classical deities or mythological figures were commonly used as decorative motifs. A bronze head of Mercury from Sandy (fig. 58) may have been attached to a leather garment. Also from Sandy, the base of the broken handle of a bronze jug shows another head, possibly of Medusa (fig. 59).

Two particular features of Celtic religion seem to have survived into the Roman period — veneration of the head and of water.[2] Springs were often centres of religious attention in the Iron Age, and votive offerings were commonly thrown into them. Their recognition as sacred places continued in Roman times, as at Bath, where the temple to Sulis Minerva was constructed over the hot mineral springs. Each spring probably had its own local deity who was believed to control the flow of water, and was therefore owed homage. A spring between Chalgrave and Toddington may have been attributed to such a deity, as in the stream nearby an intaglio ring was found, possibly thrown in as an offering (fig. 60). The engraving is of the Greek hero, Achilles, shown with a crudely carved helmet and spear, and the ring is therefore quite likely to have belonged to a Roman soldier. From Shirrell Spring, near Totternhoe, coins and pottery fragments may again bear witness to the existence of a sacred site.[3] Venus figurines from Roxton suggest a shrine near the confluence of the Ouse and Ivel rivers.[4] The connection of the water cult with a head

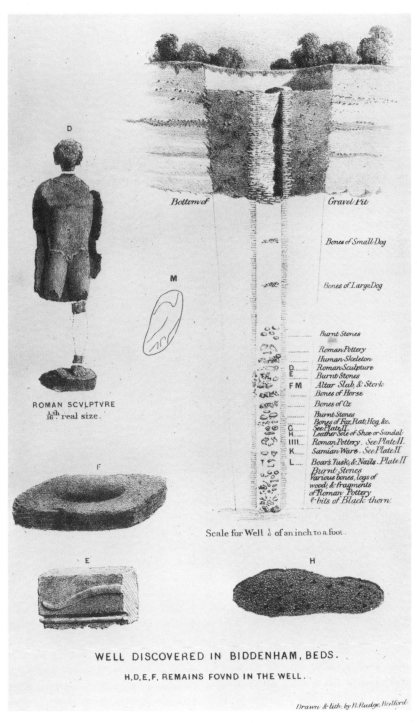

56. Well at Biddenham (G23), as originally published by W. Monkhouse.

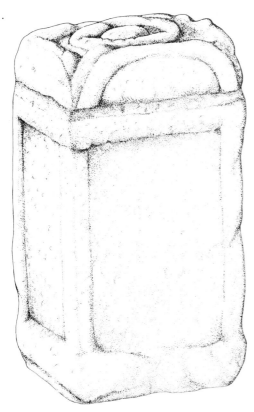

57. Portable stone altar, Kempston, G125. Scale 1:2.

59. Fragment of bronze handle with head, possibly of Medusa, Sandy, G217. Scale 1:1.

cult can be seen at the Odell farmstead, where the severed head and neck of a woman was deliberately placed behind the wicker lining of a well.[5]

Wells or ritual shafts?

Because of the religious associations connected with water supplies, some writers, especially those of the last century, were keen to ascribe a ritual function to any wells which were found, particularly the very deep shafts on the chalk hills of south Bedfordshire. It was argued that a shaft such as the one found near Maiden Bower in 1859, during the

58. Bronze plaque with head of Mercury, Sandy, G210. Width 72 mm/2.8 inches. (Copyright Cambridge University Museum of Archaeology and Anthropology).

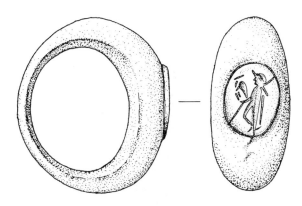

60. Intaglio ring, Chalgrave, G53. Scale 2:1.

construction of the Leighton Buzzard-Dunstable railway branch line, could not have been a domestic well; it was said to be far too deep — at least 120 feet (36 metres) — and spring water was available just down the hillside.[6] The debris in the well (animal bones, pottery and burnt stones) was assumed to be a ritual offering.

There is no reason to attribute any particular religious significance to the construction of these wells; as an engineering exercise it was quite within the technological capacity of the inhabitants of Roman Britain. Indeed, the large numbers which have been identified in Dunstable since the Manshead Archaeological Society began their rescue work in 1964 shows that they were a common feature in Durocobrivis,[7] and were clearly considered far preferable to collecting rainfall, or carrying water a distance from the nearest spring.

On the other hand, burying objects as a ritual offering was a feature of the religious beliefs particularly of late Roman Britain. Disused wells might form a suitable receptacle, although in the case of most wells, particularly those in Dunstable, the contents are usually no more than would be expected from general household refuse. Wells could also provide a convenient dumping-ground for the debris from a demolished building, as may have been the case at Biddenham. There is of course always the possibility that a well which served as a rubbish pit might also on occasions have been used to receive a ritual deposit.

Religious offerings were sometimes placed in purposely dug pits. The hoard of ironwork[8] and the group of bronze bowls (see fig. 39)[9] from Sandy may have been deposited in this way. While they might conceivably have been buried for temporary safe-keeping, there may never have been any intention of recovering them. The ironwork, for example, has sometimes been identified as a smith's hoard, but if this were the case it is strange that there are no blacksmith's tools in it.

Superstitions probably played a significant part in the lives of most people, and charms or amulets were popular. A bronze winged phallus from Totternhoe,[10] with a ring for suspension, may have been a pendant. An intaglio ring from Ruxox[11] bears the inscription "Bonus eventus" (equivalent to "Good luck"). A shark's tooth, apparently associated with a Roman cremation burial near Leighton Buzzard,[12] may also have been a good luck charm.

Religions from the East

Religious beliefs tended to travel quite freely throughout the Roman world. Often they were spread by the movement of the army, and particularly by the auxiliary troops who came from other provinces of the empire. Several variants of eastern religions came to Britain by this means, and one is attested by a recent find from Dunstable. A pot found with a skeleton in the Roman cemetery in Friary Field had an inscription round the base, which reads, in translation, "Regellinus presented the pot of the dendrophori of Verulamium".

"Dendrophori", or branch-bearers, were associated with the cult of the Syrian goddess Cybele, and were responsible for carrying a pine tree to her temple on the annual festival. They were organised into guilds made up of carpenters and woodworkers and it is thought that the pot from Dunstable represents a funerary offering from the Verulamium guild to one of its members.[13] Clearly exotic religions had found their way into the area, probably through Verulamium, where a triangular temple may have been dedicated to Cybele,[14] and where adherents from Durocobrivis could have participated in the annual rites. The skeleton which the pot accompanied was that of a young man, aged between 16 and 20 years, who was presumably a carpenter or woodworker by trade.

Christianity had probably found its way into Britain by the 2nd or 3rd century, but evidence of it was slight because official disapproval tended to drive it underground. After the conversion of Constantine in AD 312, and the Edict of Milan of 313 (which granted freedom of worship to the Christian church), official persecution ceased, and Christian symbolism tends to be encountered more frequently in the archaeological record, mainly on villa sites. However, evidence of the practice of Christianity in the Roman period in Bedfordshire is slight. An intaglio ring found at Sandy in the 18th century was said to bear a picture of the crucifixion, with a worshipping figure on each side, and engraved "In hoc signo vincas".[15] This phrase, meaning "in this sign may you conquer", was reported by early church historians as having appeared in a vision or dream to the emperor Constantine, along with the image of a flaming cross, which led to his conversion. It was widely adopted as a Christian motto. Unfortunately the ring itself has been lost, and the description cannot be confirmed.

Burial

Further insights into the religious outlooks of the Roman period can be gained by looking at the rites of burial. Belief in an afterlife was common to the Celtic and Roman religions; both pre-Roman and Roman burials were furnished with goods to provide for the needs of the deceased. The nature of these offerings remained very much the same after the conquest as before. Comparison between the Belgic-style burials at Stanfordbury[16] and the later 1st century cemetery at Shefford[17] reveals many similarities, possibly indicating a family connection as well as continuing fashion. Among the types of finds common to both sites were quantities of imported samian vessels and wine amphorae, bronze dishes and jugs, and glassware. Lower down the social scale, the pottery found in cremation cemeteries at Biddenham[18] and Kempston[19] shows that they originated in Belgic times, but continued in use into the Roman period. That at Kempston may have perpetuated an even earlier use of the site. Among vessels from the area were some overhanging rim urns of Bronze Age date, and it is likely that the late Iron Age cemetery was established on or near a Bronze Age barrow.

From the middle of the 2nd century, cremation was gradually replaced by inhumation. This probably represents changing fashion, rather than any particular alteration in religious belief, as offerings for the dead were still made. At Sandy, this change from cremation to inhumation was demonstrated by the discoveries made at Tower Hill, where both burial rites were identified. Cremation burials were found in complete pots, with other pottery vessels accompanying them, while elsewhere in the quarry, workmen described a mass of inhu-

61. *Infant burial, Newnham, G13.*

mations as "a bank of bodies".[20] Two lead coffins (see page 47) came from the same cemetery, which clearly was in use for a long time. In rural areas, burial does not seem to have been so well regulated. At Odell,[21] for example, several inhumation burials were found in the tops of disused quarry pits, the bodies presumably being disposed of as conveniently as possible. At Newnham, the skeleton of an infant was found in a shallow grave in the yard, very close to the building with a hypocaust (fig. 61). This apparently casual burial was probably a reflection of the high rate of infant mortality, rather than a measure of disrespect.

The most complete information on burial practices during the later Roman period in Bedfordshire comes from the cemetery in the south-west quadrant of Dunstable.[22] It was defined by a rectangular ditched enclosure, although by no means all the enclosure was used. There were chalk-cut graves within the enclosure, orientated mostly north-west/south-east, but other burials were cut into the fill of the ditches. Some were coffin burials, identified by the presence of coffin nails and occasionally by wood fibres. A few were probably marked in some way, as post-holes were found within or near the graves. Several burials were accompanied by offerings: a girl of

about 8 to 10 years old was buried with a bag or box of jewellery — bronze and shale bracelets, a pin and chain of bronze, a jet pin and beads, as well as large numbers of glass, stone and amber beads, with necklace clasps. Another teenage girl was wearing bracelets and finger rings. Several graves contained groups of hobnails, showing that the occupants were buried in, or with, their boots. Others were accompanied by pottery vessels, including the inscribed pot mentioned above. There does not seem to have been any social distinction between the burials within the enclosure and those in the ditches. Offerings and coffin burials are known from both.

An interesting feature of the Dunstable cemetery is the large number of decapitated skeletons — 11 out of a total of 117 recently published; all were adults, 5 male and 6 female. The decapitation does not seem to have been administered as a form of execution. If the cemetery contained a cross-section of the community which it served, a proportion of 1 in 10 as convicted criminals seems a little high. It would be most unusual to find equal numbers of male and female victims; the medieval gallows cemetery discovered on one of the Five Knolls barrows[23] on Dunstable Downs shows a male/female ratio of nearly 5 to 1, and there is no reason to suppose that Roman women were any more criminally inclined than their medieval counterparts. Two of the decapitated skeletons were accompanied by pottery vessels, and two were buried in coffins; they were therefore not complete social outcasts. Decapitation is known in many Roman burials in Britain. Usually it can be shown to have occurred after death, in connection with some little understood belief or ceremony. Perhaps it was believed to be a means of subduing the spirits of the deceased, or had some connection with the head cult mentioned above.

The spread of Christianity through Britain had its influence on burial customs. Offerings were no longer given to the dead, which makes it difficult to establish the date of the burials, and orientation became more consistently east-west. Lime or gypsum was sometimes employed as a form of embalming.[24] At Dunstable, differential decay was noted in twelve skeletons,[25] and this seems to have been due to the presence of quicklime. One of the skeletons was beheaded, and three others accompanied by gravegoods, so it is unlikely that the use of quicklime was connected with any Christian practices.

Chapter 7

ROADS AND TRACKWAYS

The study of Roman roads has attracted more attention than perhaps any other subject connected with Roman Bedfordshire. A considerable impact has been made by the work of the "Viatores" (the Latin word for travellers), published in 1964. Much of the network of Roman roads which they proposed for the Bedfordshire area has not survived detailed examination; a discussion of this can be found in the Appendix on page 78. The following roads are those which can be shown to have been constructed in Bedfordshire during the Roman occupation (see figs. 7 and 66).

Watling Street

Watling Street (the modern A5 trunk road), was laid out very soon after the conquest. It linked the Thames crossing with that of the Trent, and later with the legionary fortresses at Wroxeter and Chester, passing through the town of Verulamium where the *civitas* capital of the Catuvellauni was set up. It served as a supply route and line of communication to the frontier forces, and particularly to the XIVth legion which may have been based for a time somewhere near the junction of Watling Street with the Fosse Way south-west of Leicester.

The character of the road demonstrates how the Roman military engineers could overcome problems of terrain, but would at the same time adapt to local conditions if necessary. As it passes through Bedfordshire, the road does not follow a completely straight route, but is built up in a series of fairly short straight lengths. Clearly the engineers, in planning the section north of Verulamium, decided

to take advantage of a natural gap through the Chilterns at the point where Durocobrivis was to grow up. The gap is in the form of a dry valley which is slightly curved as it cuts through the hills south-east of Dunstable, and the line of the road followed this curve, as the A5 still does. There was no advantage to be gained by cutting the road in a more direct line through the steep chalk slopes east of Kensworth, though the Viatores argue that this is what happened.[1]

North of Dunstable the road goes over,

62. *Watling Street, looking south-east towards Dunstable. Puddlehill, where the road now runs through a modern cutting, is in the foreground, the curving earthwork to the right is the 18th century coach road, which avoided the steep hill. (Cambridge University Collection: copyright reserved).*

rather than round, the high chalk ridge now known as Puddlehill (fig. 62). The extent of the Roman engineering works on the hill cannot now be reconstructed; the present cutting is the culmination of many campaigns of work over the last 150 years. North of Puddlehill, the road, in a series of very small changes of line, curves round slightly to the west towards Magiovinium. The embankment along which this section of the road runs is of modern origin. As late as the 17th century, the road was often impassable as it ran by Hockliffe, and was at one point very low-lying.[2]

Watling Street was one of the trunk roads of Roman Britain and, as such, it would certainly have been provided with milestones. In the earlier period these were round or oval stone columns from four to six feet high, inscribed with the name and titles of the emperor in whose reign they were erected, together with a mileage figure from the nearest major town. Later, when the road was remade or repaired, they were either replaced by new stones or recut to take a new inscription; and this sometimes resulted in a squarer shape. None has so far been positively identified in Bedfordshire, and they may all have been put to later use, for example as the columns of church crosses or gateposts, but they should be looked for; and the fact that they were sometimes used as boundary marks in the post-Roman period suggests that particular attention should be paid to cases where early property boundaries join the road at intervals of one Roman mile (1618 yards or 1480 metres).[3]

Baldock-Sandy-Godmanchester

The road from Baldock to Sandy was also constructed very early in the Roman period (see page 18) and served as a by-road of the route which linked London with the legionary fortress at Lincoln. As the road enters the county from the south-east, it is followed by the line of the modern A1. At Biggleswade, however, the modern road leaves the Roman route to cross the River Ivel. This no doubt happened because the line between Biggleswade and Sandy crosses low-lying ground, liable to flood, and during the post-Roman period the unrepaired Roman road had become impassable.

There are few traces of this road between Biggleswade and Sandy, and a considerable stretch was probably obliterated when the railway was built. Towards the settlement at Sandy, the road runs

63. Roman road ditches, Cople/Willington, G278 (Cambridge University Collection: copyright reserved).

through Chesterfield, but its metalled surface was removed earlier this century because it obstructed the plough.[4] At Sandy, the alignment changes, and heads north-north-east towards Durovigutum (Godmanchester), making use of a gap in the sandstone ridge north-east of the town. The exact line can be traced after a few hundred yards, where it is preserved in an ancient boundary called Hasell's Hedge. This line continues through Everton parish, though partly obliterated by the World War II airfield, and the road finally leaves the county after forming the eastern edge of Little Barford parish.

Local Roads

The existence of a road running west from Sandy towards the Bedford area was first suggested by aerial photographs taken by Prof. J.K.S. St Joseph, showing a straight length of double ditch between Cople and Willington (fig. 63; see also fig. 18).[5] This feature has also been thought to be a large prehistoric ritual monument or cursus,[6] but its size and regularity make it quite unlike any others that are known.[7] Careful examination of aerial photographs covering the whole area between Sandy and Bedford has revealed that double ditches occur on the same alignment in several other places, at Cardington,[8] and immediately west of the Ivel.[9] While its interpretation as a Roman road seems fairly certain, it displays some peculiarities. As it approaches the complex cropmarks between Cople and Willington it stops abruptly, only to reappear again on the same alignment on the other side (fig. 64); it is difficult to imagine that a military or civil road constructed by the Roman authorities would not be cut straight through a small rural settlement which stood in its way. Moreover, the strip of land defined by the ditches shows no sign of any metalling, which would be betrayed by lighter

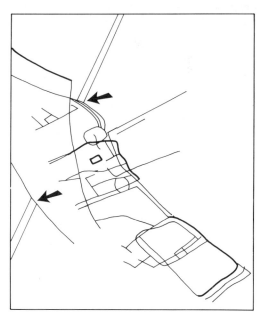

64. *Cople/Willington road, showing its relationship with the settlement cropmarks (Cambridge University Collection: copyright reserved).*

crop growth; no metalling or side ditches were detected when a gas pipe was laid across the alignment in 1976.[10] On the other hand, there is no darkening of the crop, which would indicate erosion of the surface and the creation of a hollow way through wear. It appears that the road was neither metalled, nor seriously used.

These characteristics suggest either that the road was never finished, or that it was the work of someone other than the central authorities. If the latter, then the most likely candidate is a member of the local aristocracy, who would have both the financial resources, and control of the land over which the road was laid out. It may be an example of a native leader adopting a Roman fashion as a mark of status, although economic considerations may also have played a part. Perhaps the local dignitary had a "town" house in Sandy, or an interest in its commercial life. The connection with the Ouse valley to the west would have been important, both for the supply of agricultural produce, and for access to the pottery-producing sites south-east of Bedford. Why then was the road never metalled, nor driven right through the Cople-Willington settlement? Perhaps, indeed, it was never finished, or more probably it simply failed to attract traffic, as no doubt a line of communication along the open, flat valley had been established long before.

There is also evidence of a tendency in some places to construct short lengths of straight ditched roads as part of, and in the immediate vicinity of, rural settlements. At the Cople-Willington complex (see fig. 18), as well as the road running east to Sandy there are several other regular parallel ditches leading from the main enclosures. At Astwick (fig. 65), the cropmarks of a possible villa are linked to the Baldock-Sandy road by a pair of very straight parallel ditches. There are no signs that these features continued as longer distance routes; they are probably just a symptom of the fashion, especially on higher status sites, for redesigning settlements and their fields according to a regular "Romanised" pattern.

Trackways

Clearly the large number of settlements and their interconnected economic relationships required a far more complex network of communications than the few roads of Roman origin listed above. It was not necessary however for a complete road system to be constructed from scratch after the Roman conquest. The Iron Age landscape already had its network of communications, and it is to this that we must look if we are to understand the Roman situation.

Some long-distance routes, such as the

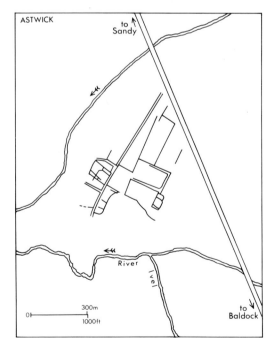

65. *Cropmarks, Astwick (G8), near the Sandy-Baldock Roman road.*

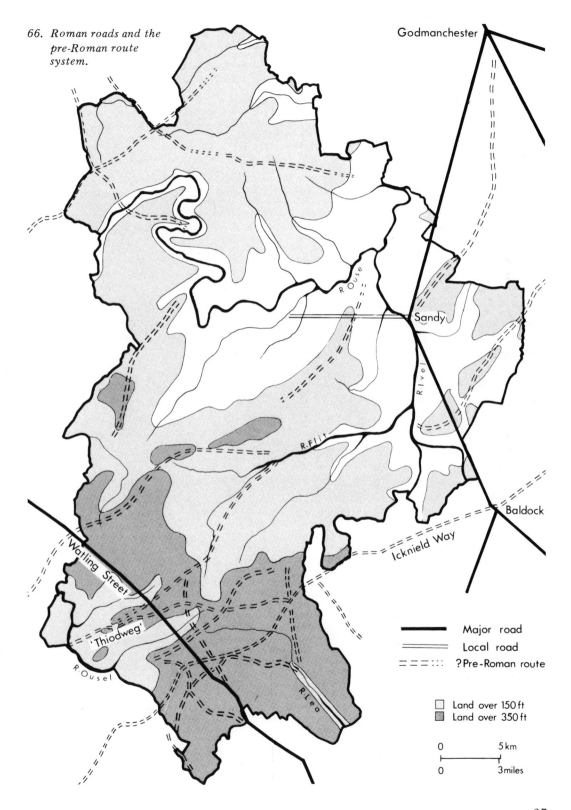

66. *Roman roads and the pre-Roman route system.*

Godmanchester

Sandy

R.Ouse

River

Baldock

R.Flit

Icknield Way

Watling Street

'Thiodweg'

R.Ousel

R.lea

Major road
Local road
? Pre-Roman route

☐ Land over 150 ft
▧ Land over 350 ft

0   5 km
0   3 miles

Icknield Way, are known to have existed since neolithic times, not as narrowly defined roads but as broad belts of communication. Throughout the prehistoric period, as communities became less self-sufficient and more dependent on trade networks, so these lines of communication increased in number and complexity. As the demand for land grew, particularly during the Iron Age, so the belts narrowed, and became trackways linking settlements to their neighbours, and to the outside world. The origin of any road or track is extremely difficult to date, but many which survive today may have a greater antiquity than previously suspected, and may go back even to prehistoric times.[11]

Some short lengths of ancient trackway can be identified from aerial photographs, where they appear as meandering double ditches. None known in Bedfordshire cover any great distances however, and they do not give any clues to the broader network. Ditches were probably only dug where the track passed through arable land, to keep travellers or stock away from the crops, and were not considered necessary on the land between farmsteads. For example, at Odell (see fig. 9), a clearly defined track runs through the fields attached to the settlement, but there are no signs that the ditches continued beyond the main arable area.

An important feature of long-distance prehistoric routes is that they were closely determined by topography. This can be clearly seen in the Icknield Way, which hugs the northern slope of the chalk hills running from central southern England to East Anglia. Steep slopes were avoided where possible, and the continuous line of hills provided an aid to route-finding which was important for any traveller in an age before maps. In attempting to identify other prehistoric routes, the

starting point is therefore to examine the natural corridors which are offered by the lie of the land. The most obvious are the river valleys which dissect the county; they were on the whole favoured areas for settlement, and would have seen a reasonable amount of local and regional traffic.

Away from the river valleys, there are probably other features like the Icknield Way which have survived as part of the modern landscape. Analysis of the earliest communications network which can be reconstructed from historical information reveals a number of tracks which closely follow topographical features (fig. 66). Some follow ridge-tops, such as that which runs south-west/north-east along the watershed between the Ouse and Nene valleys in north-west Bedfordshire, or "Thiodweg", a road joining the Icknield Way with the Ousel valley, referred to in a charter of AD 926.[12] Others follow the contours of the valley sides, or climb over high ground to link one valley to the next. Their prehistoric origin is almost impossible to prove, but it may be that they are the vestigial remains of a communications network which was in existence by the closing years of the Iron Age. If so, they probably still only comprise a fraction of the routes which had developed before the Roman invasion. But they suggest that, with river valleys forming low-lying corridors, and ridgeways linking one corridor to the next, the late Iron Age landscape was well served by connections between one settlement and another, from one area to the next.

The continuity in the settlement pattern between the late Iron Age and Roman periods has already been discussed. The communications which formed an integral part of that settlement pattern would have been equally enduring. Superimposed on this pattern after the Roman conquest came the major engineered roads, functioning in much the same fashion as a modern motorway, providing a long-distance means of official communication, but having little effect on the existing local system. There was no need to build a complex network of new straight roads across the landscape — the existing Iron Age arrangements were perfectly functional, and quite adequate for local needs.

Chapter 8

THE TWILIGHT YEARS

The decline of Roman Britain, and the arrival and eventual ascendancy of the Saxons, was a long-drawn-out process. The north and west frontiers of the province were always troublesome to the Roman authorities, with periods of peace alternating with phases of unrest, as the natives of unconquered territories flexed their muscles against the border garrisons. From the east, the first raids by Germanic tribes across the North Sea may have taken place as early as the end of the 2nd century. Throughout the 3rd and early 4th centuries, this external danger grew, and the Roman defences were strengthened along the south and east coasts, under the control of a new military commander, the Count of the Saxon Shore. A crisis was reached in AD 367, when a combined assault by Picts from Scotland, Scots from Ireland, and Saxons, left Britain in chaos. Troops deserted, and many slaves escaped in the confusion. Marauding bands seeking plunder roamed the countryside, and order was restored only when the emperor Valentinian sent Theodosius in 368 to round up the intruders, offer an amnesty to the deserters, and restructure the provincial garrison.

The 4th century was paradoxically a period of great prosperity for Britain, when villas in particular were refurbished and rebuilt on a scale of unprecedented luxury, as was the Totternhoe villa (see page 25).[1] But the external dangers could not be held at bay for ever. Towards the end of the century, a series of political and military crises marked the point of no return for the province. Pressures from the northern frontiers of the empire were beginning to threaten the security of Rome itself, and the defence of Britain fell further and further down the list of imperial priorities. A climax came in AD 383, when Magnus Maximus, the military leader of Britain, rebelled against the emperor. He crossed into Gaul, taking vital troops with him and left the British defences seriously weakened. It was not until AD 399 that central control was finally restored. However, as soon as 401, troops were again being withdrawn for the defence of Italy.

By AD 406, the danger was very serious indeed, when massive numbers of barbarians crossed the Rhine frontier of the empire. The response from Britain came through two more rebels, Marcus and then Gratian, who both took the title of emperor in Britain, presumably hoping to secure its defence by maintaining its military independence. Their successor, Constantine III, had wider ambitions. Whether he was not content with power over Britain, or whether he genuinely felt that the safety of the province was inextricably tied up with security in Gaul, he crossed the channel with his troops. Although successful in Gaul for a while, he had removed the last hope Britain had of military assistance from Rome. Constantine was defeated by the emperor Honorius, and his officials in Britain thrown out by the native leaders, but no more troops could be spared to replace the British frontier garrisons. The last official contact from Rome may have been a letter from Honorius in 410, advising the British leaders to look to their own defence.[2]

The years following 410 are obscured in the half-legend, half-history of early chroniclers.[3] Political and military leadership in Britian fell to a number of kings, of whom the names Vortigern, Ambrosius and Arthur have come down to us. The legend runs that Vortigern invited Germanic mercenaries to Britain to provide a defence against their countrymen across the North Sea, and against the Picts; they rose in rebellion and plundered and slaughtered the native British. Ambrosius, and then Arthur, campaigned against the invaders, eager to restore the golden days of Roman rule, and a temporary respite was achieved at the battle of Mount Badon c. AD 500. But in 571, Cuthwulf won a final victory over the British at *Biedcanford* (not to be identified with Bedford[4]), and captured four settlements in the southern midlands, including *Lygeanburg* (Limbury).

The reality behind the legend was far more complex. For example, Germanic mercenaries had been officially employed by the Roman army long before the early 5th century, and archaeological evidence from eastern England suggests they were already attached to Roman settlements before the final break with Rome. Whoever Vortigern was, his policy of settling mercenaries in Britain was only the continuation of a long-established practice. The Saxon domination of England was not a sudden event, but a gradual takeover. The mercenaries grew in number, probably augmented by their families, at the same time as the whole structure of Roman civilisation in Britain was breaking down.

Slowly the balance of power swung, at first in localised areas, then more generally, and the great names and battles recorded in history were only some of the highlights in a whole spectrum of shifting fortunes. No doubt there were attacks and massacres; but there must also have been periods of coexistence. Native leaders, with the right connections, may well have made their way to the comparative security of the west, but we have no reason to believe that the British-speaking inhabitants were totally ousted or exterminated. However, the numbers of invaders were sufficient to bring about in the long term a complete change of language, except for a few surviving Celtic river and place names. The remaining British hung on in isolated enclaves, and then perhaps as slaves, but were finally absorbed, and the heritage of the Roman civilisation which had collapsed about their ears became little more than a memory.

With the historical background still so little understood, can the archaeological evidence from Bedfordshire shed any light on the end of the Roman occupation? There are many problems in interpreting that evidence, particularly in reconstructing the last days of the settlements, villas and farmsteads. For most of the Roman period, pottery styles and coins are helpful in chronicling the history of settlements. Towards the end, these aids are not available. The supply of coinage declined dramatically at the end of the 4th century; what coins there were continued in circulation longer than had previously been usual, until the use of coins was abandoned altogether at some time during the 5th century. The great centres of the pottery industry collapsed suddenly, as the economy failed and the distribution networks were disrupted. The mass-produced wares were replaced by home-made vessels, difficult to identify and date, or by wood and leather containers. The last coin on a site or the latest fragment of datable Nene valley tableware do not therefore necessarily give the date at which that site was abandoned. Occupation of a site may appear to come to an end at the close of the 4th century, but it may be that the signs of continuing occupation have just not been recognised.

In trying to reconstruct the end of the Roman period in Bedfordshire there are two lines of enquiry. Analysing the evidence of unrest, and the desertion of settlements, may present a picture of the decline of Romano-British society, and the loss of its population; the remains left by the earliest Saxon settlers should indicate when they arrived and where they were based. Comparison of these two sources of information may give some clues as to how and when the Saxon takeover occurred.

There are no signs in Bedfordshire of widespread destruction of Roman settlements, as would be expected if the Saxon invasion had been a once-for-all event, involving the massacre of the native population. On the other hand, there is no evidence of any site continuing in unbroken occupation from the Roman to the Saxon period, which might have occurred in the course of a totally peaceful infiltration. The manner of the Saxon arrival was probably somewhere between these two extremes. There are several indicators of unrest, and of a general deterioration of living standards in the late Roman period.

The occurrence of coin hoards is usually a sign of troubled times. For example, hoards from Flitwick[5] and Podington[6] were buried c. AD 270, at a time when Saxon raids on the British coast were becoming a serious problem. Others from Cranfield[7] and Tingrith[8] (and possibly Totternhoe[9]) date from the middle years of the 4th century, when there were further signs of trouble and for a time Magnentius usurped authority in the western empire. The close of that century is marked by two hoards of silver coins found in recent years at Kempston,[10] and another possible hoard among the many coins found at Sandy,[11] all reflecting the increasing insecurity of the period.

Further signs of the troubled nature of the times can be detected in the apparent deterioration in the standards of burial recorded on several late Roman sites. The cemetery at Dunstable[12] has been discussed in some detail (see page 61). It showed the development of a tendency to bury the dead in the quickest way possible, by making use of the soft fill of the boundary ditches instead of digging laboriously into undisturbed chalk. Burials were also frequently placed in the tops of disused wells. In the modern cemetery at Sandy,[13] a Roman pit was uncovered which contained three skeletons buried head first, possibly also dating from the 4th century. Around the barrows of the Five Knolls on Dunstable Downs,[14] and on Galley Hill, Streatley,[15] late Roman interments were made in shallow graves and with little sign of ceremony. At Newnham,[16] the fragmentary remains of a skeleton were uncovered lying just below the surface of the late Roman yard; it is unlikely that this would have happened if it had still be in active use as a villa farmyard.

There is no reason to believe that any of these burials represent victims of the Anglo-Saxons. It is more probable that they are a sign of a general collapse of morale among the British population, as they were struggling to cope with the failure of the way of life they had known. The economic basis of their prosperity was shattered. The industries which supplied their basic equipment were folding up, or at least they were unable to distribute their products because the trade networks no longer functioned. The coins which had been a mark of financial prosperity were becoming worthless as people no longer had confidence in them. Agriculture had to continue, but always under the threat of the last ploughshare breaking with no replace-

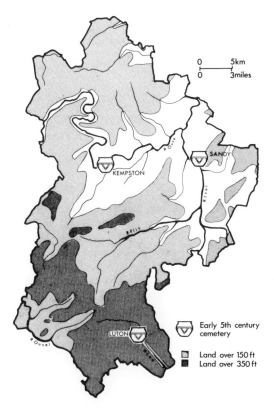

67. The earliest Saxon evidence.

were. Dunstable was perhaps deserted early — it seems to have had no urban defences, and its position on the Icknield Way/Watling Street cross-roads made it extremely vulnerable. Its market function ceased, and those who had made a living there through trade no longer had any reason to stay; moreover, maintenance of the water supply seems to have been abandoned, as the wells fell into disuse.[18] Many rural farmsteads probably struggled on, to be deserted through external force, or because too few people remained to run the farm.

While the Roman age was entering its twilight years, the first material remains of the Saxon newcomers appear. Pottery of the earliest Saxon type, in the form of cremation urns, has been found at Sandy,[19] Kempston[20] and Argyll Avenue, Luton[21] (fig. 67). The locations are significant. The Saxon cemetery at Sandy lay immediately north-west of the Roman settlement, slightly away from the Roman cemetery. Argyll Avenue is within a mile of the extensive Roman complex at Limbury.[22] The large Saxon cemetery at Kempston adjoins and partly overlaps the earlier Roman one,[23] and lies in the most densely occupied part of the Ouse Valley; the two silver coin hoards mentioned above were both found within about a mile of it.

Were these first Saxon newcomers here through armed invasion, or as invited "guests"? The answer can only be conjecture. In the first place it is impossible to tell whether these early remains were always specifically connected to centres of Roman population, or whether that is just where they happen to have been found so far. If the settlements did have their origins in groups of mercenary soldiers, brought in to protect late Roman settlements, then they are in the very places where they would be expected. If, on the other hand, they were the first

ment available. The climate itself may have been deteriorating, adding further stress to rural communities.[17] At times like this, elaborate and time-consuming burial practices must have had a low priority.

None of the Roman sites in Bedfordshire which have been examined in detail show any evidence of continuing much into the 5th century. However this may simply be due to the lack of datable finds. Some were no doubt deserted. Members of the higher classes who had property in the tribal capital at Verulamium would be likely to take advantage of the comparative security its defensive walls offered, leaving their country estates to function as best they could. Those without that freedom of choice would have to stay where they marauding bands, they would hardly run the risk of establishing cemeteries in close proximity to settlements of the very people they were trying to displace.

This early Saxon presence in the county shows that the battle of Biedcanford of 571 was not simply a seizure by the invaders of completely new territory. The places taken by the Saxons on that occasion (Eynsham and Benson in Oxfordshire, Aylesbury and Limbury) represent a tract of land from the Cotswolds to the Chilterns. But the early 5th century material from Luton demonstrates that the area that was captured in Bedfordshire had not been exclusively British up to that date. On the other hand, excavated evidence from Verulamium shows that the town was occupied in a reasonable degree of comfort until late into the 5th century,[24] so the British survival and the Saxon arrival clearly overlapped to a considerable extent. How this worked in practice is uncertain.

While Saxon cemeteries are easily identified, the traces of their settlements are notoriously difficult to find. Their pottery was dark and coarse, and easily disintegrates in the plough-soil. It is also very similar to early Iron Age pottery, and may on occasions not have been recognised when it has been found. A Saxon presence in the countryside can, however, be detected. At Totternhoe,[25] 5th century pottery was found in the layers of earth which were accumulating over the ruins of the villa. At Newnham,[26] early Saxon decorated sherds were found among the building rubble, and one came from a post-hole, suggesting some sort of "squatting" occupation in the Roman ruins. If, as suggested above, the villa owners were the first to find a refuge elsewhere, the villa farms may soon have become vacant land, there for the taking.

Some clues to this transition period may come in the guise of place-names, though there are so many traps for the unwary in this field that any suggestions made here are offered with extreme caution. Very few place-names can be used to shed light on this earliest Saxon period but some forms may be relevant here, namely those which make use of borrowed Latin words.[27] Some of these borrowed words have not been studied in enough detail for us to be sure of their significance. For example, the Latin word *castra* may have been applied to towns in 4th century Britain. It was adopted by the invaders as *ceaster* or *caester*, and occurs in the field name "Chesterfield", where the Roman settlement at Sandy is mainly located. It is just possible that the first Saxon settlers in the Sandy area gave it the name because they could see it still standing and functioning; on the other hand, it could have been applied much later as an umbrella term which was used in the Old English language for any substantial Roman remains.

The place-name *wicham*, incorporating the Latin *vicus*, is thought to have more definite significance. The term *vicus* probably meant a village in late Roman Britain, although it had also had a more precise administrative meaning in earlier times. Its occurrence ties in so closely with the location of Roman settlements that it has been argued that the name was only applied in the early stages of the Saxon invasion, when the newcomers knew of the *vicus* because it was still in existence. *Wicham* is preserved in field-names on the borders of Stanbridge[28] and Tilsworth,[29] where a Roman settlement is known to extend across the clay hilltop,[30] and in "Wickham Field" in Maulden[31] which lies partly over the extensive settlement at Ruxox.[32] Perhaps here we have evidence of the earliest Saxon settlers preserving in place-names the memory of the late Roman settlement which they moved in alongside.

In the 5th and early 6th century, the population in the Bedfordshire area was a mixture of the late Roman survivors and Saxon immigrants. An uneasy peace was perhaps maintained between the two groups because of the British military superiority supposedly represented by the Mount Badon victory. In settlement terms, the farmsteads of one may have alternated with those of the other, though the relative numbers of settlements and population cannot be established. Clearly nothing like the Roman way of life survived — the British inhabitants probably came to make use of Saxon products, such as their pottery, and the possessions of the different populations may have been indistinguishable. The balance of superiority however swung relentlessly in the Saxon favour. If a British farmstead failed, it was not compatriots who took it over; the drift was westwards towards non-Saxon areas, rather than in the other direction. There would be no shortage of newcomers to take up the vacant land, as the sphere of Saxon influence spread further and further west. Added to the general uncertainty facing the British population was the occurrence of natural disaster. Plague swept Europe in the 6th century, and if this took its toll in Britain, then those who stepped into the gap were Saxon, not British.

The Saxon victory of 571 did not mark a new expansion into previously untouched areas. It merely confirmed the inevitable.

POSTSCRIPT

A survey of the kind presented here can only reflect our current state of knowledge. In spite of the quantity of information represented by the 288 gazetteer entries, there remain many gaps in our understanding of Roman Bedfordshire, its history and its way of life. Some of the background is fairly clear. While our Roman predecessors in the county are, with a very few exceptions, anonymous, some of the figures on the wider stage are known, the emperors and generals, chieftains and governors. Where we have no local evidence for part of the overall picture, an outline of sorts can be sketched in by reference to what is known from similar areas elsewhere. What is lacking in the county in the way of the rich and spectacular is balanced by the many fragments of evidence which go some way towards completing the jigsaw puzzle.

Much more work can be done, even in analysing the discoveries that have been made to date. What, though, are the priorities, if we wish to expand our knowledge further? The casual finds of the last three centuries have played a large part in building up the picture; a further three centuries of casual finds, assuming the evidence lasts that long, would be most unlikely to double our understanding. The first discovery of Roman coins in the Ouse valley was a major advance of knowledge — here was evidence of Roman occupation for the first time; another handful in 1984 will tell us little more.

The general picture put forward in the preceding chapters is based on two very different, but complementary, types of information. First, there is the broad survey, where programmes of walking over large areas of countryside, ploughed field by ploughed field, have helped to revolutionise our understanding of settlement patterns, for the prehistoric as well as for the Roman period, in national as well as local terms. Some areas of the county, hitherto hardly examined, would benefit greatly from similar treatment. A related form of work is the regular monitoring of large-scale development, whether building schemes or road construction. Often this involves last minute salvage, with little hope of recovering anything but a small proportion of the evidence, but it often provides the vital information of where settlements do *not* occur, as well as where they do. These programmes of survey and rescue recording contribute to the broad picture, to the reconstruction of the Roman landscape as a whole.

Secondly, by means of the detailed investigation of particular sites by excavation, we can understand how the buildings and fields of a settlement were laid out, and how they changed over time. The complete range of surviving household goods can be analysed, to give a picture of how styles and techniques of manufacture developed over the centuries, and to demonstrate how the settlement related to the trade and commerce of its locality — what it was producing, and what was being bought from where with the resulting income. Modern scientific techniques allow a reconstruction of agricultural life, through the study of seeds and pollen, insect remains and animal bones. This level of investigation is, however, no simple matter. The project which studied the farmstead at Odell, from which much of our information on rural life in Roman Bedfordshire has come, involved nearly four years uninterrupted work in the field, and more than that again in analysing the information and finds which were recovered. This was only possible because the work was co-ordinated with a programme of gravel extraction, which dealt with most of the heavy earth-moving required to clear the site of its overburden. Such projects obviously demand a high level of resources, but once brought to completion provide a corpus of information which can be drawn upon to enhance our understanding not only of sites of a similar type, but also of the period as a whole. They are rarely undertaken, and are normally only considered when a site is already destined to destruction by some means, and when the returns of information are expected to justify the resources required.

The preservation of the Roman remains of Bedfordshire is a difficult problem. There are no upstanding Roman ruins, and the only definitely Roman sites which enjoy legal protection under the Ancient Monuments and Archaeological Areas Act (1979) are the Totternhoe Roman villa (G265), and the settlement at Cardington, scheduled because it lies within a neolithic interrupted ditch enclosure (G44). Many buried sites are only revealed when the plough slices off the upper layers and brings objects to the surface. Once this has happened it is difficult, without excavation, to assess how much of the evidence lies undisturbed, especially in areas where deep-ploughing and mole-drainage have been practised for many years. On these grounds, few rural settlements are likely to qualify for scheduling as ancient monuments. Other less typical sites must await more detailed study and survey work before they can be submitted for consideration.

The period of Roman rule in Britain lasted almost 400 years. Before the invasion, the Iron Age population was structured by political, ethnic and economic ties which, left alone, may have developed into a society almost as complex and inter-related as that stimulated by the Roman occupation. This Iron Age framework was overlain by a veneer of Roman civilisation, at first adopted only slowly by the wealthier classes, but gradually embracing the whole of British life, until Britain's fate, as a Roman province, became entirely bound up with that of her political and military masters.

With the end of Roman Britain, the influence of four centuries of Roman government was effectively eclipsed. Even those aspects of our modern culture which owe their origins to ancient Rome seem to have been re-introduced as Saxon and medieval England became more closely linked with her European neighbours. But beneath the sixteen hundred years of subsequent history can still be detected vestiges of Roman Britain — the roads refurbished, the town sites reused, the Roman brick in Saxon churches, even our modern settlement pattern, developing as it did because of the way the Saxon settlers fitted into the existing late Roman landscape. Our understanding of those vestiges, and of the part that the Roman period has played in the history of the Bedfordshire region, will never be complete. This book has attempted to offer a skeletal outline of what we have learnt since that first "urn, red like coral" came to light at Sandy over three hundred years ago. It is hoped that the survey work, rescue excavation, and chance discoveries of the coming years will put more flesh on the bones.

Appendix

ROMAN ROADS AND THE VIATORES

The Viatores suggested that there was a complex network of Roman roads in Bedfordshire, with a total length of nearly 200 miles or 320 kilometres (fig. 68a). Some parts of this were admitted to be conjectural, leaving approximately 120 miles (200 kilometres) for which evidence of some sort was put forward (fig. 68b). The features which the Viatores looked for in tracing roads included straight lengths of modern road or trackway, straight hedgerows and parish boundaries, and visible earthworks.

In analysing the Viatores' work the lines of the supposed roads have been checked against the available historical maps.[1] The most useful maps are those relating to the Enclosure Awards of the late 18th and early 19th centuries. These record the agreements whereby the old common fields were divided up and re-allocated to individual owners; as part of this reorganisation of the landscape, many new roads and tracks were laid out, and new hedgerows planted, very often in straight lines. Many of the modern roads and hedgerows which were taken by the Viatores as evidence of Roman roads were only created at the time of Enclosure, and therefore could not be Roman in origin.[2] Figure 68c shows what is left of the Viatores network (approximately 90 miles/145 kilometres) when all these stretches are removed. Only a few of the remaining lines have the appearance of Roman engineered roads (fig. 68d). Watling Street, the Baldock-Sandy-Godmanchester route, and the rather untypical road running west from Sandy have been discussed in Chapter 7. The evidence for three other stretches is inconclusive, but they could perhaps be mentioned here:

a) Woburn Park. A short length of Viatores' road no. 176[3] follows a raised drive in Woburn Park, and a section of parish boundary. A straight track is shown on this line on a map of 1661,[4] but a continuation in either direction would follow the pre-Roman alignment suggested on figure 66, rather than the Viatores' line.

b) North of Streatley, road no. 170b.[5] The Streatley place-name is one which incorporates the element *straet* (paved road),[6] and suggests there was a feature of that description in the area when the Saxon predecessor of Streatley was first named. Part of the parish boundary north of the hamlet of Sharpenhoe is very regular in its alignment. To the south, the topography dictates that any continuation would follow the line of the modern road between Sharpenhoe and Streatley village, where it climbs a slight valley in the chalk scarp. No continuation can be traced to the north. The general direction of this stretch of possible road lies between the Limbury area north of Luton and the Ruxox area, and it may represent a line of communication between the Lea and Flit valleys.

c) Goldington.[7] East of Bedford, the line of Newnham Avenue is continued in an ancient boundary running northwards through Goldington parish, giving a total of about two miles. This may, however, be a landscape division of post-Roman date, similar to the straight parish boundaries surviving on the south side of the River Ouse.

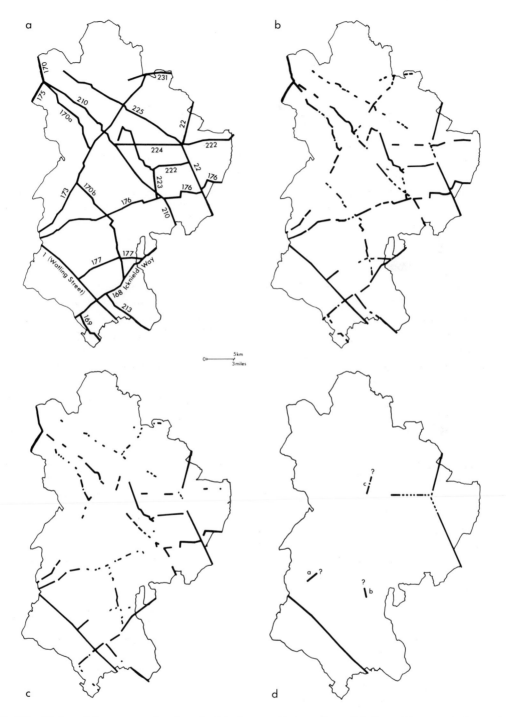

68. *The Viatores' Roman road network: (a) the complete system; (b) the evidence put forward; (c) after removal of modern features; (d) after removal of the roads which show little sign of Roman engineering.*

LIST OF ABBREVIATIONS

AASRP	*Associated Architectural Societies' Reports and Papers*
Acc. no.	Accession number
Ampthill Arch. Soc.	Ampthill and District Archaeological and Local History Society
Ant. J.	*Antiquaries Journal*
Arch.	*Archaeologia*
Arch. J.	*Archaeological Journal*
BAAS	Bedfordshire Architectural and Archaeological Society
BAR	British Archaeological Reports
Beds. Archaeologist	*Bedfordshire Archaeologist* (Journal of the South Bedfordshire Archaeological Society)
Beds. Arch. J.	*Bedfordshire Archaeological Journal*
Beds. Mag.	*Bedfordshire Magazine*
BHRS	*Bedfordshire Historical Record Society*
BNFAS	*Bulletin of the Northamptonshire Federation of Archaeological Societies*
BNQ	*Bedfordshire Notes and Queries*
Brit.	*Britannia*
Cambridge Mus.	Cambridge University Museum of Archaeology and Anthropology
CBA Gp. 9 NL	*Council for British Archaeology Group 9 Newsletter*
CRO	Bedfordshire County Record Office
CUCAP	Cambridge University Committee for Aerial Photography
G	Gazetteer entry (followed by number)
Gent's Mag.	*Gentleman's Magazine*
Inf.	Unpublished information provided by
JRS	*Journal of Roman Studies*
Manshead Arch. Soc.	Manshead Archaeological Society of Dunstable.
Manshead Mag.	*Manshead Magazine* (Journal of the Manshead Arch. Soc.)
Mus.	Museum
NMR AP	National Monuments Record Air Photographs Unit
n.s.	new series
Num. Chron.	*Numismatic Chronicle*
OS	Ordnance Survey Archaeology Record
PSA	*Proceedings of the Society of Antiquaries*
SMR	Sites and Monuments Record (followed by number)
Unprov.	Unprovenanced
VCH	*Victoria County History*

NOTES

Chapter 1

1. Quoted in Johnston, 1974, 37.
2. Lysons and Lysons, 1806, fig. 1 opposite p.24.
3. Taddy, 1853, 428 (**G211**).
4. **G20**.
5. William Stukeley, *Itinerarium Curiosum*, 1776, Centuria I, p. 78.
6. Camden, 1695, 289.
7. **G272**.
8. **G175**.
9. **G223**.
10. **G231**.
11. Fox, 1923, 204.
12. Page and Keate, 1908.
13. Gurney recorded his researches in a large number of notebooks, which are deposited mainly in the Bedfordshire County Record Office (X325) and in the collections of the Buckinghamshire Archaeological Society at Aylesbury. They have been analysed in detail by Stephen Coleman.
14. CRO: X325/110, 1917-18.

Chapter 2

1. Julius Caesar, *De Bello Gallico*, V, 14.
2. See also **G171**.
3. *op. cit.*, V, 12.
4. The drawings of pottery from Harrold are taken from B.N. Eagles and Vera I. Evison, "Excavations at Harrold, Bedfordshire, 1951-53", *Beds. Arch. J.* 5, 1970, 17-55. Those from Felmersham and Kempston are from Angela Simco, "The Iron Age in the Bedford region", *Beds. Arch. J.* 8, 1973, 5-22.
5. *op. cit.*, IV, 20-36 and V, 1-23.
6. Wheeler and Wheeler, 1936, 16-22; but this has been widely questioned recently.
7. *ibid.*, 10-16.
8. Warwick Rodwell, "Coinage, Oppida and the Rise of Belgic Power in South-Eastern Britain", in Barry Cunliffe and Trevor Rowley (eds.), *Oppida in Barbarian Europe*, BAR Supplementary Series 11, Oxford, 1976, 181-367, esp. pp. 265-271.

9. Eagles and Evison, *op. cit.* (note 4).
10. G187.
11. G231.
12. G191.
13. Mansel Spratling, "The Late Pre-Roman Iron Age Bronze Mirror from Old Warden", *Beds. Arch. J.* 5, 1970, 9-16.

Chapter 3

1. Frere, 1983, 37-44.
2. A fort of mid-1st century date is suggested by Charmian Woodfield, "A Roman Military Site at Magiovinium?", *Records of Bucks.* 20, pt. 3, 1977, 384-399.
3. See Graham Webster, *The Roman Invasion of Britain*, Batsford, 1980, Map II, p. 112. (Webster's suggestion of a fort site at Harrold cannot be confirmed.)
4. By Manshead Arch. Soc.
5. Green, 1975, 185.
6. G231.
7. G223.
8. G28.
9. E.g. Tacitus, *Annals*, XIV, 29-39.
10. Green, 1975, 185.

Chapter 4

1. Hachures have been adopted on figure 7 because at this scale contour lines cannot indicate with sufficient precision the details of the terrain in relation to the distribution of settlements. Contours are recorded on the larger scale gazetteer maps (figs. 70-76). Information for adjacent counties has been drawn from the relevant Sites and Monuments Records, and I am grateful to Mike Daniels of Hertfordshire County Council, Mike Farley of Buckinghamshire County Museum, Glen Foard of Northamptonshire County Council and Alison Taylor of Cambridgeshire County Council for their assistance. Information for Northamptonshire has also been derived from the Royal Commission on Historical Monuments inventories, *Archaeological Sites in North-East Northamptonshire*, 1975 and *Archaeological Sites in Central Northamptonshire*, 1979.
2. David Hall, personal communication.
3. G97.
4. Matthews, 1963, pl. VIb.
5. G246.
6. G90.
7. G223.
8. G258.
9. G23.
10. G47.
11. G8.
12. G231.
13. G191.

14. G154.
15. Austin, 1928, 25-26.
16. G175.
17. G174.
18. Detailed records made by the author during restoration work in the winter of 1981/82. Publication forthcoming.
19. G5.
20. G114.
21. Since this was written, the Manshead Arch. Soc. have reported the discovery of a villa in this area.
22. Maurice Beresford, *New Towns of the Middle Ages*, Lutterworth Press, 1967, 394.
23. Camden, 1695, 289.
24. See A.L.F. Rivet, "The British Section of the Antonine Itinerary", *Brit.* 1, 1970, 34-82.
25. R.W. Bagshawe in Viatores, 1964, 25.
26. G63.
27. E.g. Camden, 1695, 288.
28. Ptolemy, *Geography*, II, 3, 11.
29. Mawer and Stenton, 1926, 107.
30. Rivet and Smith, 1979, 121-122.
31. See Johnston, 1974, for a summary of the discoveries.
32. G210.
33. G211.
34. G212.
35. G216.
36. G154.
37. Manning, 1955.
38. *JRS* 47, 1957, 214.
39. Dyer and Dony, 1975, 15.
40. G174.
41. Notes in CRO: CRT 130/Flitwick/1.

Chapter 5

1. G36.
2. G97.
3. *PSA* 2, 1849-53, 109 (Mayle, E. and Price, E.B.) quoted in Johnston, 1974, 41 (G211).
4. E.g. Smith, 1904, 51 (Dunstable, exact provenance unknown); see also G270 and G120.
5. G42.
6. Matthews and Hutchings, 1972, 31 (**G63**).
7. J.P. Wild in Matthews *et al.*, 1981, 49 (**G63**).
8. Edgar Lovatt, *Beds. Mag.* 3, 1951-3, 223.
9. *Beds. Mag.* 7, 1959-61, 100 (**G174**).
10 Manning, 1964, 55 (**G217**).
11. Johnston, 1974, 39 (**G212**).
12. E.g. Odell, **G187** (report by Annie Grant on animal bones in Dix, 1983 forthcoming.)
13. Matthews *et al.*, 1981, 71 (**G63**).
14. Luton Museum acc. no. 415/39 (**G164**).
15. OS: letter from John Morris, 1954 (**G265**).
16. E.g. Bletsoe, **G32** (*Bedford Modern School*, 1936, 84); Radwell, **G90** (Hall, 1973, 69).
17. Matthews and Hutchings, 1972, 23 (**G63**).

18. G154.
19. *JRS* 47, 1957, 214.
20. G104.
21. G36.
22. G15.
23. G79.
24. G45.
25. G13, unpublished pottery analysis by Pat Aird.
26. G259.
27. James Wyatt, *PSA* (2nd series) 6, 1873-6, 184.
28. Maj. W. Cooper Cooper, *PSA* (2nd series) 10, 1883-5, 134.
29. G156.
30. Manning, 1955, 22 (**G154**).
31. G246.
32. Johnston, 1974, 47 (**G211**).
33. Taylor and Woodward, 1982 forthcoming, fig. 3, no. 23 (**G207**).
34. G231.
35. Frere, 1972, 80-81.
36. Matthews and Hutchings, 1972, 27 (**G63**).
37. Taddy, 1853, 427 (**G211**).
38. *JRS* 47, 1957, 214 (**G154**).
39. Matthews *et al.*, 1981, 60 (**G63**).
40. Johnston, 1974, 43 (**G217**).
41. CRO: X325/53, Gurney notebook, 1913-14 (**G260**).
42. Steward, 1898, 14-15 (**G104**).
43. Dix, 1983 forthcoming (**G187**).
44. G201.
45. CRO: X69/16, *BAAS Minute Book*, p.110 (11 Nov. 1851) (**G128**).
46. G38.
47. Watkin, 1882, 270 (**G210**).
48. G66.
49. G54.
50. Johnston, 1974, 40 (**G211**).
51. *ibid.*, 45 (**G217**).
52. Hall and Nickerson, 1966; Hall and Hutchings, 1972.
53. *Bedford Modern School*, 1936, 84 (**G32**).
54. Hall, 1973, 71 (**G90**).
55. Matthews and Hutchings, 1972, 26-27 (**G63**).
56. *CBA Gp. 9 NL* 2, 1972, 20 (**G174**).
57. E.g. Sandy, **G217** (Manning, 1964, 55).
58. Matthews and Hutchings, 1972, 27 (**G63**).
59. Manning, 1964, 51-53 (**G217**).
60. *ibid.*, 53 (**G217**).
61. Matthews and Hutchings, 1972, 27 (**G63**).
62. E.g. *Manshead Mag.* 14, Dec. 1964, 5 (**G64**).
63. Brown, 1972, 8 (**G104**).
64. R.S. Baker, *AASRP* 13, pt. 1, 1875, 110 (**G215**). Sir William Peel in fact died of smallpox at Cawnpore in 1858, seven weeks after receiving a bullet wound in the thigh at the Lucknow siege (Sir Leslie Stephen and Sir Sidney Lee (eds.), *The Dictionary of National Biography*, Oxford University Press, 1967-8, vol. 15, 670.
65. G231.
66. Johnston, 1974, 46.
67. Hall, 1973, 71 (**G90**).
68. Matthews *et al.*, 1981, 44 (**G63**).
69. G191.
70. Matthews *et al.*, 1981, 45 & pl. 2b (**G63**).
71. G47.
72. G186.
73. Johnston, 1974, 39 (**G210**).
74. G97.
75. G150.
76. G265.
77. G246.
78. G14.
79. G258.
80. G13.
81. G104.
82. *Bedford Modern School*, 1936, 84 (**G32**).
83. E.g. Elstow, **G87**.
84. Dyer and Dony, 1975, 15 (**G154**).
85. G218.
86. See Steward, 1898, 14-15.
87. See e.g. Pliny, *Natural History*, XXXIV, 31. I am grateful to Mark Hassall for his comments on the oculists' stamps, and to Stanley Warren for directing me to the classical literature.

Chapter 6

1. See Martin Henig, *A Corpus of Roman Engraved Stones from British Sites*, BAR 8, Oxford, 2nd edn., 1978, 198 & pl. IV no. 102. I am grateful to Dr Henig for drawing his description to my attention.
2. See Anne Ross, *Pagan Celtic Britain*, Routledge, 1967.
3. G266.
4. Taylor and Woodward, 1982 forthcoming (**G207**).
5. G187.
6. G121.
7. E.g. **G63**, **G64**.
8. G217.
9. G215.
10. G273.
11. Ampthill Arch. Soc., 1973, 3 (**G174**).
12. G147.
13. M.W.C. Hassall in Matthews *et al.*, 1981, 46 & 48; *Brit.* 11, 1980, 406-407 (**G63**).
14. Wheeler and Wheeler, 1936, 113-120.
15. *England Illustrated: or, a Compendium of the Natural History, Geography, Topography and Antiquities Ecclesiastical and Civil of England and Wales*, 1764, quoted in *Gent's Mag.* 34, 1764, 60 (**G210**).
16. G231.
17. G223.
18. G25.
19. G125.
20. CRO: X69/16 *BAAS Minute Book*, p. 143

(8 Jul. 1853) (**G211**).
21. **G187**.
22. **G63**.
23. See **G75**.
24. See Christopher J.S. Green, "The significance of plaster burials for the recognition of Christian cemeteries" in Richard Reece (ed.), *Burial in the Roman World*, Council for British Archaeology Research Report 22, London, 1977, 46-53.
25. Matthews *et al.*, 1981, 7.

Chapter 7

1 Viatores, 1964, 24-31 (R.W. Bagshawe, R.H. Reid).
2. Stephen R. Coleman, *Hockliffe: Historic Landscape and Archaeology*, Bedfordshire County Planning Department, 1983, 37.
3. I am grateful to Prof. A.L.F. Rivet for his comments on milestones.
4. Johnston, 1974, 35 (**G210**).
5. Johnston, 1956, 95.
6. See James Dyer's review of Viatores, 1964, in *Beds. Mag.* 9, 1963-5, 216-218, esp. p. 218.
7. Roy Loveday, personal communication.
8. E.g. NMR AP: TL 0848/4/16 (6 Aug. 1975).
9. Hunting Surveys Ltd: HSL UK 76 31, run 7/2291-2 (3 Jul. 1976).
10 Marion Barnett, personal communication.
11. See Christopher Taylor, *Roads and Tracks of Britain*, Dent, 1979.
12. Gurney, 1920, 163.

Chapter 8

1. **G265**.
2. Though many scholars now believe the letter refers to Bruttium in south Italy, not to Britain.
3. Such as the *Anglo-Saxon Chronicle*; Bede, *Historia Ecclesiastica Gentis Anglorum (An Ecclesiastical History of the English People)*; Gildas, *Excidio et Conquestu Britanniae (On the Ruin and Conquest of Britain)*; Nennius, *Historia Brittonum (History of the Britons)*.
4. Comparison with other place-names (e.g. Bakewell, Derbyshire, which was Badecanwelle in Old English spellings) shows that Biedcanford could not have become Bedford; as this type of name alters over time it is always the *d* and not the *c* which disappears. (I am most grateful to Dr Margaret Gelling for her detailed comments on this point.)
5. **G98**.
6. **G202**.
7. **G61**.
8. **G257**.
9. **G272**.

10. **G128** (inf. Bedford Mus., 1978); **G126**.
11. Johnston, 1974, 47 (**G217**).
12. **G63**.
13. Johnston, 1974, 39 (**G212**).
14. **G75**.
15. **G240**.
16. **G13**.
17. See Hubert H. Lamb, "Climate from 1000 BC to 1000 AD", in Martin Jones and Geoffrey Dimbleby (eds.), *The Environment of Man: the Iron Age to the Anglo-Saxon Period*, BAR 87, Oxford, 1981, 53-65, esp. pp. 57-58.
18. E.g. Matthews *et al.*, 1981, 11-13 (**G63**).
19. Sources summarised in Audrey Meaney, *A Gazetteer of Early Anglo-Saxon Burial Sites*, George Allen and Unwin, 1964, 39-40.
20. David H. Kennett, *The Anglo-Saxon Cemetery at Kempston, Bedfordshire: A Reconsideration*, unpublished thesis, 1968.
21. William Austin, "A Saxon Cemetery at Luton, Beds.", *Ant. J.* 8, 1928, 177-192.
22. **G154**.
23. **G125**.
24. Frere, 1983, 23-25 & 226.
25. **G265**.
26. **G13**.
27. See Margaret Gelling, *Signposts to the Post*, Dent, 1978, 63-74.
28. The name "Wickham Slade" is recorded in several 17th century references in the CRO, of which the earliest traced is a post-nuptial settlement of 1623 (GA 2669).
29. The earliest known reference is to "Wickham Hill" in 1608. I am grateful to Joan Schneider for drawing this to my attention (publication forthcoming).
30. **G233**.
31. CRO: MA 32 and Book K, Maulden Enclosure Award, 1797.
32. **G174**.

Appendix

1. I am particularly grateful to the staff of the CRO for their assistance in making the maps available for inspection.
2. Detailed notes by the author, analysing the Viatores' roads within Bedfordshire, have been deposited in the CRO. For a discussion of a particular length of road, illustrating the problems involved, see John Wood, *Kempston: Historic Landscape and Archaeology*, Bedfordshire County Planning Department, 1984.
3. Viatores, 1964, 287 (R.W. Bagshawe).
4. CRO: X1/33.
5. Viatores, 1964, 295 (R.W. Bagshawe).
6. Mawer and Stenton, 1926, 164.
7. Viatores, 1964, 349 (R.W. Bagshawe).

BIBLIOGRAPHY

General Reading

A. Birley, *Life in Roman Britain*, Batsford, 1976.

R.G. Collingwood and Ian Richmond, *The Archaeology of Roman Britain*, Methuen, 1969.

Sheppard Frere, *Britannia: a history of Roman Britain* (2nd edn.), Routledge & Kegan Paul, 1969.

Joan Liversidge, *Britain in the Roman Empire*, Routledge & Kegan Paul, 1968.

Ivan D. Margary, *Roman Roads in Britain* (3rd edn.), John Baker, 1973.

Ian Richmond, *Roman Britain* (2nd edn.), Penguin, 1963.

A.L.F. Rivet (ed.), *The Roman Villa in Britain*, Routledge & Kegan Paul, 1969.

A.L.F. Rivet, *Town and Country in Roman Britain* (2nd edn.), Hutchinson, 1964.

Peter Salway, *Roman Britian*, Oxford University Press, 1981.

Malcolm Todd, *Roman Britain 55 B.C. – A.D. 400*, Fontana, 1981.

John Wacher, *Roman Britain*, Dent, 1978.

Cited Works

Ampthill Arch. Soc., *Flitwick: A Short History*, Ampthill Arch. Soc., 1973.

Austin, William, *The History of Luton and its Hamlets*, Newport, I.O.W., 1928, vol. 1.

Bagshawe, Richard W., "A search for the site of Durocobrivae – Part I", *Beds. Archaeologist* 2, 1959, 21-26.

Bedford Modern School Field Club Journal and Museum Bulletin 3, Nov. 1936, 83-84, "Excavations on a Romano-British Site at Bletsoe", Anon, but almost certainly F.W. Kuhlicke.

Blundell, Joseph Hight, *Toddington: Its Annals and People*, Toddington, 1925.

Brandreth, Henry, "Observations on the Roman Station of Magiovintum", *Arch.* 27, 1838, 96-108.

Brown, A.E., "Roman Pottery Kilns at Harrold Bedfordshire 1970", *Milton Keynes Journal of Archaeology and History* 1, 1972, 7-9.

Camden, William (ed. Edmund Gibson), *Britannia*, 1695 (David & Charles facsimile).

Catherall, P.D., Barnett, M., McClean, H. (eds.), *The Southern Feeder: The Archaeology of a Gas Pipeline*, British Gas, forthcoming.

Davis, Frederick, *The History of Luton with its Hamlets*, Luton, 1855.

Dix, Brian, "Excavation at Harrold Pit, Odell, Bedfordshire 1974-1978", *Beds. Arch. J.* 17, 1983 forthcoming.

Dryden, Sir Henry, "Roman and Roman-British Remains At and Near Shefford co Beds.", Cambridge Antiquarian Society quarto publication, 1845.

Dyer, James and Dony, John G., *The Story of Luton*, White Crescent Press, Luton, 3rd edn., 1975.

Fadden, Kevan, "A Field-Walking Exercise in the Ampthill Area", *Beds. Arch. J.* 10, 1975, 1-4.

Fox, Cyril, *The Archaeology of the Cambridge Region*, Cambridge University Press, 1923.

Frere, Sheppard, *Verulamium Excavations*, Society of Antiquaries Research Reports 28 and 41, London, vol. I, 1972 and vol. II, 1983.

Green, H.J.M., "Roman Godmanchester", in Warwick Rodwell and Trevor Rowley (eds.), *Small Towns of Roman Britain*, BAR 15, Oxford, 1975, 183-210.

Gurney, Frederick G., "Yttingaford and the Tenth-Century Bounds of Chalgrave and Linslade", *BHRS* 5, 1920, 163-178.

Hagen, Richard, "A Roman Ditch in Dunstable Priory Meadow", *Beds. Arch. J.* 7, 1972, 35-38.

Hall, D.N., "Rescue Excavations at Radwell Gravel Pits, 1972", *Beds. Arch. J.* 8, 1973, 67-91.

Hall, D.N. and Hutchings, J.B., "The Distribution of Archaeological Sites between the Nene and the Ouse Valleys", *Beds. Arch. J.* 7, 1972, 1-16.

Hall, D.N. and Nickerson, N., "Sites on the North Bedfordshire and South Northamptonshire border", *Beds. Arch. J.* 3, 1966, 1-6.

Hutchings, J.B., "Milton Ernest – A Field Survey", *Beds. Arch. J.* 4, 1969, 69-78.

Inskip, T., "On Ancient Relics Collected in Bedfordshire", *AASRP* 1, pt. 1, 1850, 165-172.

Johnston, David E. (1956), "A Romano-British Site near Bedford", *Beds. Archaeologist* 1, 1955-6, 92-97.

Johnston, David E., "The Roman Settlement at Sandy, Bedfordshire", *Beds. Arch. J.* 9, 1974, 35-54.

Kennett, David H. (1970), "The Shefford Burial", *Beds. Mag.* 12, 1969-71, 201-203.

Langdon, Rev. Percy G., *Bedford Modern School Museum: Illustrated Guide*, Bedford, 1925.

Lysons, Rev. Daniel and Lysons, Samuel, *Magna*

Britannia, vol. 1, 1806.

Manning, William H. (1955), "A Roman Site at Runfold Avenue, Limbury", *Beds. Archaeologist* 1, 1955-6, 21-27.

Manning, W.H., "A Roman Hoard of Ironwork at Sandy, Bedfordshire", *Beds. Arch. J.* 2, 1964, 50-57.

Matthews, C.L., "Archaeological Sites of the Totternhoe Ridge", *Manshead Mag.* 8, Apr. 1962, 118-134.

Matthews, C.L., *Ancient Dunstable: A Prehistory of the District*, Manshead Arch. Soc., undated, but 1963.

Matthews, C.L. and Hutchings, J.B., "A Roman Well at Dunstable", *Beds. Arch. J.* 7, 1972, 21-34.

Matthews, C.L. and Members of the Manshead Archaeological Society, "A Romano-British Inhumation Cemetery at Dunstable", *Beds. Arch. J.* 15, 1981, *passim*.

Mawer, A. and Stenton, F.M., *The Place-Names of Bedfordshire and Huntingdonshire*, English Place-Name Society, vol. 3, Cambridge University Press, 1926.

Monkhouse, W., "An Enquiry into the site of the Roman Station 'Durocobrivae' ", *AASRP* 5, pt. 2, 1860, 281-289.

Page, William and Keate, Miss, "Romano-British Bedfordshire", *VCH Beds.* 2, 1908, 1-15.

Peacock, D.P.S., "Roman Amphorae in Pre-Roman Britain", in David Hill and Margaret Jesson (eds.), *The Iron Age and its Hillforts*, University of Southampton Monograph Series No. 1, 1971, 161-188.

Ransom, William, "An Account of British and Roman remains found in the Neighbourhood of Hitchin", *Transactions of the Hertfordshire Natural History Society* 4, 1886, 39-48.

Richmond, Robert, *Leighton Buzzard and its Hamlets*, Leighton Buzzard, 1928.

Rivet, A.L.F. and Smith, Colin, *The Place-Names of Roman Britain*, Batsford, 1979.

Smith, Worthington G., *Man the Primeval Savage*, Edward Stanford, London, 1894.

Smith, Worthington G., *Dunstable: Its History and Surroundings*, 1904 (reprinted by Bedfordshire County Library, 1980).

Steward, William, *Glimpses of the History of a Bedfordshire Village* [Harrold], Bedford, 1898.

Taddy, Rev. John (1853), "On the Roman and Saxon Remains lately disinterred at Sandy, Bedfordshire; and some Remarks on the Roman Settlement in Britain", *AASRP* 2, pt. 2, 1852-3, 422-432.

Taylor, Alison and Woodward, Peter, "Excavations at Roxton, Bedfordshire, 1971-74: The post-Bronze Age Settlement", *Beds. Arch. J.* 16, 1982 forthcoming.

The Viatores, *Roman Roads in the South-East Midlands*, Victor Gollancz, 1964.

Watkin, W. Thompson, "Roman Bedfordshire", *Arch. J.* 39, 1882, 257-290.

Wheeler, R.E.M. and Wheeler, T.V., *Verulamium: A Belgic and Two Roman Cities*, Society of Antiquaries Research Report 11, London, 1936.

White, R.F., "The Bedford Southern Orbital Sewer: a watching brief", *Beds. Arch. J.* 14, 1980, 19-24.

LOCATIONS OF OBJECTS ILLUSTRATED

BedM = Bedford Museum. CM = Cambridge University Museum of Archaeology and Anthropology. LM = Luton Museum and Art Gallery. LSM = Longsands School Museum, St Neots.

Fig. 1: BedM BM 89. *Fig. 2:* BedM 3278. *Fig. 4:* a, BedM, b, BedM BM1 and 3644. *Fig. 13:* LM 339/40. *Fig. 20:* a, BedM; b, BedM 66/B/114. *Fig. 21:* LM 14/269/53. *Fig. 22:* BedM 3509. *Fig. 23:* Manshead Archaeological Society. *Fig. 24:* LSM. *Fig. 25:* BedM 69/B/155. *Fig. 27:* BedM. *Fig. 28:* a, BedM 3296; b, BedM 3307; c, BedM 3289; d, BedM 3301. *Fig. 29:* a, BedM 65/B/722; b, BedM 3319; c, BedM 3379; d, BedM. *Fig. 30:* BedM BM 15. *Fig. 31:* BedM 65/B/722. *Fig. 32:* BedM 3404-5. *Fig. 33:* British Museum. *Fig. 34:* a, LM 1982/61; b, BedM 3345; c, BedM; d, LM 27/42. *Fig. 35:* a-b, BedM; c-d, LSM; e, BedM. *Fig. 36:* a, LM BL/269/39; b, LM 268/52. *Fig. 37:* a, LSM; b-c, BedM. *Fig. 38:* BedM. *Fig. 39:* BedM 3298-3300. *Fig. 40:* CM 65.81. *Fig. 41:* CM 1886.25. *Fig. 42:* LM L4. *Fig. 43:* BedM 69/B/154. *Fig. 44:* BedM 12761. *Fig. 45:* BedM. *Fig. 46:* a, LM 2/281/53; b, LSM. *Fig. 47:* LSM. *Fig. 48:* CM 83.765.I.3. *Fig. 49:* a, BedM 3711; b, BedM. *Fig. 50:* BedM. *Fig. 52:* BedM. *Fig. 53:* BedM 3402. *Fig. 54:* LSM. *Fig. 55:* LM A1. *Fig. 57:* BedM 3292. *Fig. 58:* CM 23.127. *Fig. 59:* BedM 3401. *Fig. 60:* LM 95/49.

GAZETTEER

This gazetteer has to be selective for reasons of space. The entries have therefore been limited on the whole to those sites where the quantity and nature of the finds suggest the existence of a settlement. Unprovenanced finds have been omitted unless they are of intrinsic interest or clearly represent a settlement somewhere in the locality (e.g. Higham Gobion, G116); some numbered entries will therefore not appear on the gazetteer maps. Material with only a general provenance (identified by "*c*" in the gazetteer entry) is shown in the centre of the most likely area. Isolated single finds, the majority of which are coins, have not been included.

Each entry follows a standard format, with the description followed by a general location by national grid reference (where known). The grid references are limited to four figures, in order to safeguard the security of the sites listed. Only the main sources of information are included, which will usually be the first known references. Where the primary sources are specialist or rare publications, more widely available secondary sources are also mentioned for the benefit of the local readership. Detailed information and sources for each site, and for those items not included in the gazetteer, are held in the Sites and Monuments Record and the SMR number is given at the end of each entry.

There are no Roman remains in the county which are visible above ground. The great majority of the sites in the gazetteer lie beneath farmland, and are not accessible to the public. Those readers wishing to visit a Roman site in the area are referred to the Roman town at Verulamium (St Albans). Bedford Museum (Castle Lane, Bedford) and Luton Museum (Wardown Park, Luton) both have displays of Roman finds, some of which are illustrated in the preceding pages.

AMPTHILL (Map C)

1. A group of pottery kilns was uncovered during the construction of the Ampthill bypass in 1982. Salvage excavation showed them to be Belgic in origin, but continuing in production into the early Roman period.
   TL 0236.
   Inf. Ampthill Arch. Soc.
   SMR 6743.
2. A ditch containing 1st century pottery was revealed during the construction of the Ampthill bypass in 1982.
   TL 0237.
   Inf. Ampthill Arch. Soc.
   SMR 4448.
3. Pottery scatter, located by field-walking.
   TL 0438.
   Fadden, 1975, 2-3.
   SMR 1429.

ARLESEY (Map E)

4. At Etonbury, where substantial earthworks (now much damaged) were probably medieval in origin, the laying of a sewage pipe in 1972 produced some Roman pottery.
   TL 1937.
   Inf. D.C. King.
   SMR 395.

5. Large quantities of 1st and 2nd century samian and other pottery in William Ransom's collection. (See page 29).

> Unprov.
> Page and Keate, 1908, 4.
> SMR 1893.

ASPLEY GUISE (Map C)

6. Pottery found in 1958 during digging of house foundations.

> SP 9335.
> Aspley Heath School Historical Society (revised and enlarged by Scholars of Fulbrook Secondary School), *A History of our District*, 1962, 10.
> SMR 11246.

ASPLEY HEATH (Map C)

7. An amphora was found in a sandpit on Wavendon Heath (now in Aspley Heath parish) several years before 1806. It is of 1st century south Spanish origin, and probably came from a Belgic or early Roman wealthy burial. (See page 8 and fig. 2).

> Unprov.
> Lysons and Lysons, 1806, 483 & fig. 4 opposite p. 24; Peacock, 1971, 165 & 182.
> SMR 864.

ASTWICK (Map E)

8. Cropmarks of a very regular layout are almost certainly Roman, and may represent the site of a substantial building or villa. The settlement is linked to the Baldock-Sandy Roman road by a 400 metre length of straight ditched track. (See pages 28 and 66, and fig. 65).

> TL 2238.
> CUCAP; NMR AP.
> SMR 3550.

9. Ten 2nd century samian vessels found during coprolite digging before 1886. They may have come from G8.

> Unprov.
> Ransom, 1886, 40.
> SMR 503.

BARTON in the CLAY (Map G)

10. Occupation site, producing early Iron Age, Belgic and Roman pottery, located by field-walking.

> TL 0832.
> Inf. D. Hall, 1978.
> SMR 9352.

11. Scatter of Iron Age, Roman and Saxon pottery, located by field-walking.

> TL 0930.
> Inf. D. Hall, 1978.
> SMR 9354.

12. Pottery found in Han Furlong; site dug as army training exercise during World War II.

> TL 0931.
> Inf. I.J. O'Dell, 1980.
> SMR 11982.

BEDFORD (Map D)

Some early antiquaries asserted that Bedford was Roman in origin but this is clearly not the case. The alleged British name of the town ("Liswider" or Lettidur") was arrived at simply by translating "bed" and "ford" into the supposed Celtic equivalent, and has no basis in fact. There have also been occasional references to Bedford being the Roman "Lactodorum" (presumably because it sounds something like "Lettidur"), but Lactodorum is actually at Towcester on the Watling Street. A healthily sceptical discussion of this subject can be found in F.W. Kuhlicke, "The Antiquity of Bedford", *Beds. Archaeologist* 1, 1955-6, 5-8.

The confusion has been in part perpetuated by reports of a "Roman villa" having been found in Castle Lane in 1881 (Watkin, 1882, 274n2; Page and Keate, 1908, 5). The reference, to "Roman bricks, fragments of flues, and tesselated work, and encaustic tiles, having in them Norman and perhaps Saxon mouldings" is extremely ambiguous. Modern excavations in the same area have found no traces of a villa or other Roman building; the few abraded Roman sherds found there, and on other sites in the centre of Bedford, are no more than would be expected in any part of the river valley. (See David Baker, Evelyn Baker, Jane Hassall and Angela Simco, "Excavations in Bedford 1967-1977", *Beds. Arch. J.*

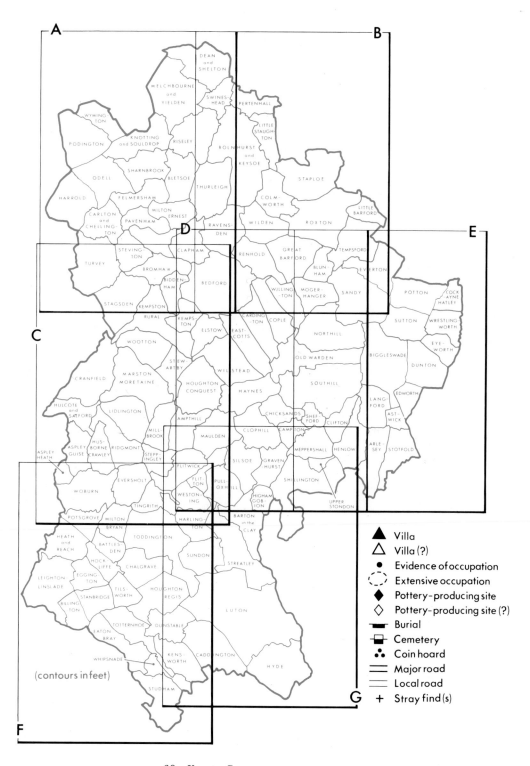

Villa △

Villa (?) △

Evidence of occupation ●

Extensive occupation ◌

Pottery-producing site ◆

Pottery-producing site (?) ◇

Burial ▬

Cemetery ⊟

Coin hoard ⁝

Major road ══

Local road ─

Stray find(s) +

(contours in feet)

69. Key to Gazetteer maps.

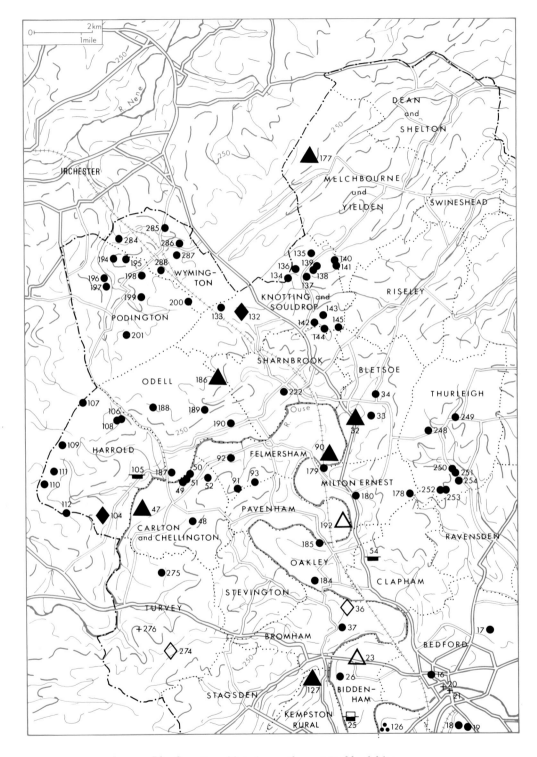

70. *Gazetteer Map A: north-west Bedfordshire.*

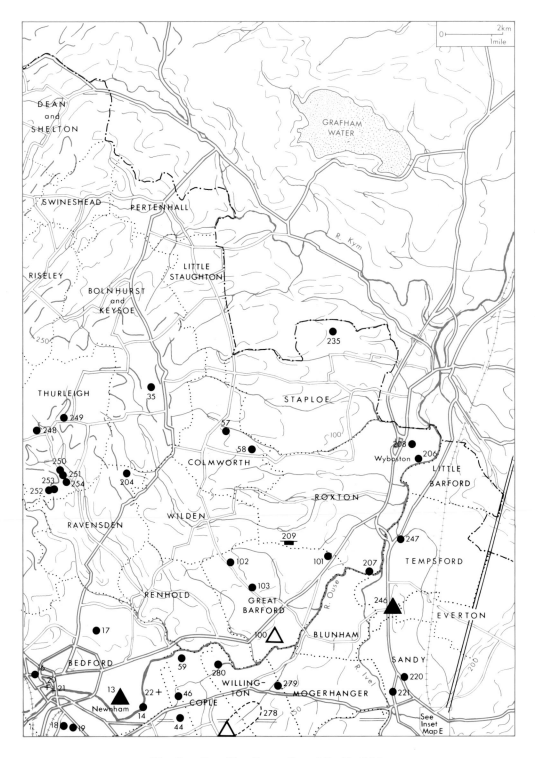

71. Gazetteer Map B: north-east Bedfordshire.

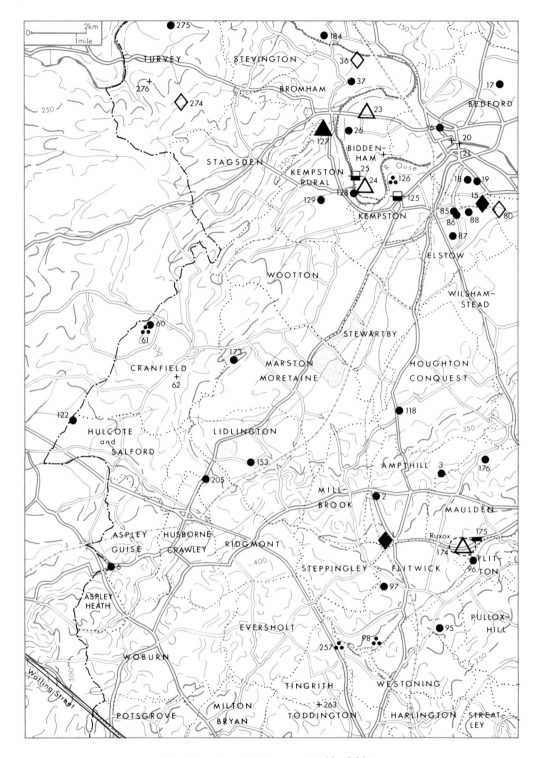

72. Gazetteer Map C: west Bedfordshire.

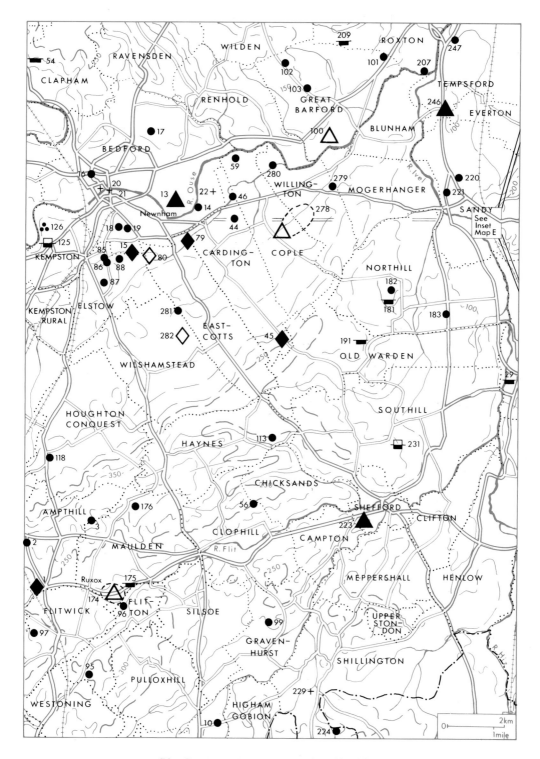

73. Gazetteer Map D: central Bedfordshire.

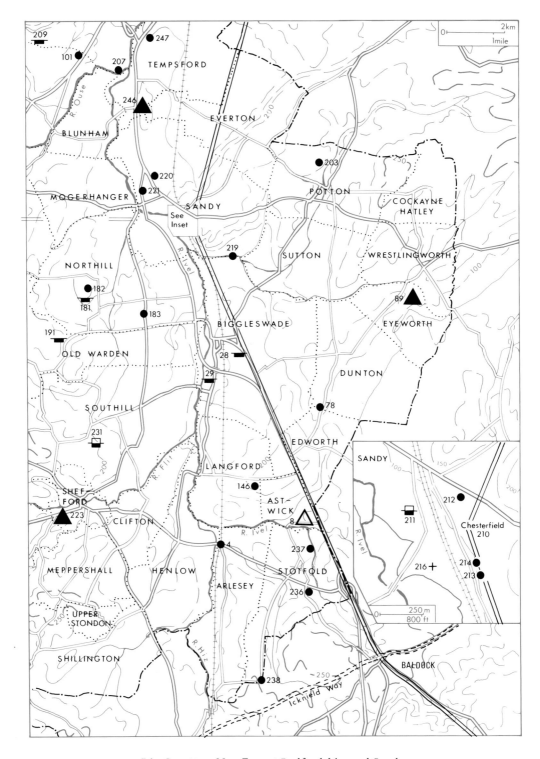

74. *Gazetteer Map E: east Bedfordshire and Sandy.*

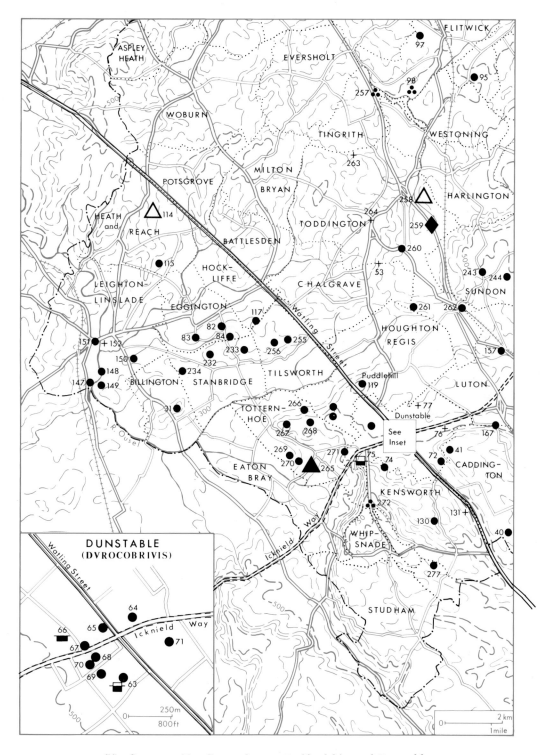

75. *Gazetteer Map F: south-west Bedfordshire and Dunstable.*

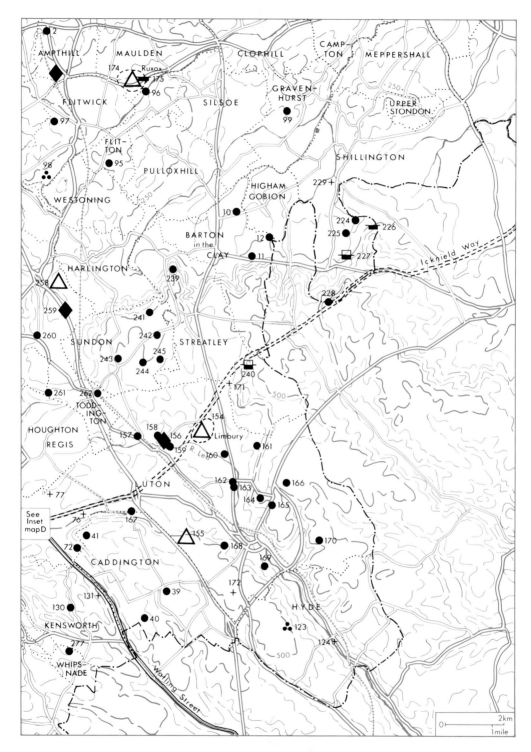

76. Gazetteer Map G: south-east Bedfordshire.

13, 1979.) This does not negate the possibility that the river crossing was in use in Roman, or even prehistoric, times.

13. At Newnham, a villa set in a rectilinear field system. Part of the complex was destroyed by gravel quarrying in the 1950s, and the rest in the 1970s. Rescue excavations in 1972-5 located fragmentary building foundations, with a hypocaust system probably representing the remains of a bath-house. The settlement had its origins in the early Roman period, and Saxon pottery in the yard area shows some kind of occupation in the early post-Roman period. (See pages 26, 40, 46, 53, 61, 72 and 74, and figs. 14, 15, 35a & b, 37b & c, 38, 45, 52 and 61.)

TL 0749.

CUCAP; Johnston, 1956, 92-94; *Beds. Arch. J.* 8, 1973, 139; 10, 1975, 80-81; 11, 1976, 84; *Brit.* 4, 1973, 296; 5, 1974, 435; 6, 1975, 256; 7, 1976, 335; *CBA Gp. 9 NL* 3, 1973, 17; 4, 1974, 9; 5, 1975, 17; 6, 1976, 17.

SMR 986.

14. A small excavation in 1958 on an area of rectilinear cropmarks uncovered a few features of Iron Age date, with a spread of Roman pottery. The construction of the Bedford Southern Orbital Sewer through the site in 1977 produced building materials, probably indicating a farmstead site. A lime kiln of 2nd century date was also located, suggesting a phase of building construction about that time. (See page 52).

TL 0848.

CUCAP; David E. Johnston, "Excavation at Newnham and Mill Farm, Bedford", *Beds. Archaeologist* 2, 1959, 16-19; R.F. White, "A Roman Lime Kiln Near Cardington Mill, Bedford", *Beds. Arch. J.* 12, 1977, 23-26.

SMR 302.

15. A pottery production site has been excavated by G. J. Dring in Mile Road. Occupation began in the Belgic Iron Age, with the production of grey ware beginning as the use of more Romanised pottery fabrics developed. The building of John Bunyan School in an adjacent area, where cropmarks had been photographed, revealed enclosure ditches of Belgic and Roman date. (See page 40).

TL 0547-0647.

CUCAP; *Beds. Arch. J.* 4, 1969, 85;

G.J. Dring, "Romano-British pottery kiln site near Elstow", *Beds. Arch. J.* 6, 1971, 69-71; G.J. Dring, "A pre-Roman and early Romano-British settlement near Bedford", *Beds. Arch. J.* 7, 1972, 81-82.

SMR 979.

16. While extending a Victorian house on Bromham Road in 1884, workmen found "a stratum . . . which displayed very clear traces of the action of fire . . . a large quantity of broken pottery . . . . The sides of the excavation were lined with large stones and some Roman tiles. Both of these, and the associated clay, and a substance resembling concrete at the bottom, had clearly been subjected to intense heat . . . There appeared to be a central mass of limestone and clay, about two feet across, bounded on either side by flue-like spaces, more than twelve inches wide. The clay, stones, etcetera, forming the sides of these spaces were more especially baked . . . ". T.G. Elger suggested it was a place where bodies were cremated, but it may have been either part of the hypocaust system of a substantial building or villa, or possibly a pottery kiln.

TL 0450.

T.G. Elger, *Beds. Times and Independent,* 14 Apr. 1894, p.3; Page and Keate, 1908, 5.

SMR 249.

17. Roman pottery and a pewter plate found during housing development at Putnoe in the 1950s. (See figs. 25 and 43).

TL 0651.

Inf. Bedford Mus.

SMR 1909.

18. A small jar and other pottery fragments from Piercey Road.

TL 0548.

Inf. Bedford Mus.

SMR 270.

19. Frequent finds of Belgic and Roman pottery during building development off the London Road.

TL 0548.

Inf. Bedford Mus.

SMR 271.

20. Excavations for Charles Wells' brewery in Horne Lane in 1887 produced an assortment of finds of which only a coin of Diocletian (AD 284-305) was definitely Roman. Supposed "Roman" pottery (now in Bedford Museum) is medieval. (See page 8).

TL 0449.

T.G. Elger, *PSA* (2nd series) 12, 1887-9, 115-116; T.G. Elger, "Ancient Bedford", *BNQ* 3, 1893, 97-102, esp. pp. 100-102; Page and Keate, 1908, 5.

SMR 293.

21. Coins of Nerva (AD 96-98), Hadrian (AD 117-138) and Faustina (mid-2nd century) were discovered when the old Bedford bridge was taken down in 1811.

TL 0549.

CRO: P1/1/10, St Paul's Parish Register, 1810-12; Page and Keate, 1908, 5.

SMR 286.

22. The lower half of a quern of Hertfordshire conglomerate (fig. 20b) was found on Corporation Farm, Cardington (actually within Bedford parish).

c. TL 0849.

Inf. Bedford Mus.

SMR 12779.

BIDDENHAM (Map C)

23. A stone-lined well was discovered in 1857 during gravel digging. It was 40 feet (12 metres) deep, and contained pottery, animal bones, a human skeleton, fragments of sculpture and a "cartload of pebbles". It has attracted various interpretations from a "sepulchre" in Monkhouse's original report to a "ritual shaft" (James Dyer, *Beds. Arch. J.* 11, 1976, 17), but it need not necessarily be regarded as anything other than a domestic well, associated with an unrecorded farmstead in the vicinity. The presence of altar fragments and parts of the sculptures of a bird and a human torso suggests a settlement of some wealth, though there is a lack of the debris which would be expected from a substantial building. The use of a well for the disposal of human remains is typical of the burial practices of the late Roman period. (See pages 27-8, 35 and 56, and fig. 56).

TL 0150.

Rev. W. Monkhouse, "On the Well at Biddenham, Beds.", *AASRP* 4, pt. 2, 1858, 283-290; Page and Keate, 1908, 5-6.

SMR 330.

24. Surface finds of pottery (including samian sherds and colour-coated ware), coins and fragments of flue tiles probably represent a substantial building.

TL 0148.

Inf. E. Compton, 1983.

SMR 3663.

25. Mid-19th century gravel extraction in South Field, Biddenham, regularly produced quantities of Belgic and early Roman pottery, including urns containing cremations. This may represent a cemetery attached to G24. (See page 60).

c. TL 0148.

James Wyatt, *PSA* (2nd series) 3, 1864-7, 304; Watkin, 1882, 285; Page and Keate, 1908, 5-6.

SMR 325.

26. Pottery and coins have been found on arable land west of Biddenham.

TL 0150.

Inf. Bedford Mus.; E. Compton, 1983.

SMR 323.

27. A gold ring, and silver and bronze coins, were found by E. Compton in 1980. The ring bore the lettering EVSEBIO VITA, meaning "long life to Eusebius". (See page 42 and fig. 33).

TL 0249.

Catherine Johns, "A Roman gold ring from Bedford", *Ant. J.* 61, 1981, 343-345; *Brit.* 13, 1982, 411.

SMR 10308.

BIGGLESWADE (Map E)

28. A bronze patera, with a fluted handle with ram's head terminal, was found during housing development in the 1960s. It is of a type which was imported from Italy in the 1st century AD, and probably came from a burial. (See pages 18 and 46-7, and fig. 40).

TL 1944.

David H. Kennett, "A Roman patera from Biggleswade", *Beds. Arch. J.* 4, 1969, 82-83.

SMR 916.

29. Inhumation burial found in the significantly named Coffin Close before 1864, with a bronze lamp, and one vessel each of glass and pottery. (See pages 46-7 and fig. 41).

TL 1843.

CRO: X69/16, *BAAS Minute Book,* p. 351 (17 May 1864).

SMR 5216.

30. 1st and 2nd century Roman brooches have been found by Mr S. W. George in the R. Ivel.

Unprov.

Seen and identified at the British Mus., 25 Jan. 1978.

SMR 11261.

An oculist's stamp claimed to have come from Biggleswade, has been demonstrated in Johnston, 1974, 46-47 to have been found at Sandy, G218. See also SANDY, G219.

BILLINGTON (Map F)

31. Roman pottery (including colour-coated ware), found in trial excavations on the site of

an Iron Age hillfort on the crest of a ridge, suggests some re-use of the site in the Roman period.

> SP 9422.
> *Manshead Mag.* 2, Jan. 1959, 17.
> SMR 528.

BLETSOE (Map A)

32. When foundations were being dug for a new rectory in August 1936, skeletons and Roman coins were discovered. Excavations by F.W. Kuhlicke produced evidence, in the form of tiles and tesserae, which suggested a substantial building in the vicinity. Work by North Bedfordshire Archaeological Society, and later by Christina Colyer concentrated on an inhumation cemetery, which cut through late Roman levels and may have been of middle Saxon date. The bulk of the finds from the site are of the later Roman period, and comprise large quantities of pottery and many coins, with some evidence of iron-smelting. (See pages 36n16, 48 and 53).

> TL 0258.
> *Bedford Modern School*, 1936; *Beds. Arch. J.* 4, 1969, 85; 5, 1970, 119 & 121; 6, 1971, 82; *Brit.* 2, 1971, 267.
> SMR 307.

33. Several acres of occupation, located by field-walking.

> TL 0258.
> Hall and Hutchings, 1972, 9.
> SMR 2637.

34. A dense scatter of pottery, all of the first half of the Roman period, located by field-walking.

> TL 0259.
> Inf. A.E. Brown, C.C. Taylor, 1980.
> SMR 2642.

BOLNHURST and KEYSOE (Map B)

35. Large quantity of Roman pottery on the site of an earthwork (probably prehistoric) at Manor Farm; located by field-walking, 1982.

> TL 0859.
> Inf. A.E. Brown, C.C. Taylor.
> SMR 315.

BROMHAM (Map A)

36. A Belgic and Roman occupation site close to the river was investigated by P.G. Tilson in 1970-2 prior to gravel extraction. Features recorded include ditches, gullies and pits, traces of circular huts, a drying oven and occupation layers. "Kiln debris, including wasters" suggests production of pottery, which has been named "Clapham shelly ware", but no kilns were located. Occupation appears to have ceased in the 3rd century, and the site was subsequently subjected to flooding. (See pages 33 and 39, and fig. 27b).

> TL 0252.
> Peter Tilson, "A Belgic and Romano-British site at Bromham", *Beds. Arch. J.* 8, 1973, 23-66.
> SMR 975.

37. Pottery and a file.

> TL 0151.
> OS (F.W. Kuhlicke, 1957).
> SMR 599.

38. Bronze steelyard weight found in 1853. (See page 45).

> Unprov.
> John Pickford, *Notes and Queries* (9th series) 7, Apr. 1901, 317; Page and Keate, 1908, 6.
> SMR 8568.

CADDINGTON (Map G)

39. In describing a "Romano-British land surface" at Buncer's Farm, cut into in 1895, Smith refers to a "heap of flint chips and tools, a stone axe or two and an arrowhead . . . two bronze Roman coins, a small piece of Roman millstone and several pieces of Roman pots". This seems an unlikely collection, and probably a scatter of Roman finds had been mixed with a prehistoric flint-working area.

> TL 0619.
> Smith, 1904, 56-57.
> SMR 86.

40. "Roman urns, some at first entire", reported from the brickfields south of Caddington.

> TL 0518.
> Smith, 1904, 52.
> SMR 87.

41. Early Roman pottery collected from an area of somewhat indistinct cropmarks.

> TL 0321.
> CUCAP: inf. R. Hagen, 1976.
> SMR 1778.

42. Roman quern rough-out from Blows Downs. (See page 34).

> Unprov.
> Smith, 1904, 54.
> SMR 1156.

CAMPTON (Map D)

43. Amphora.
> Unprov.
> Langdon, 1925, 53, pl. 13.
> SMR 381.

CARDINGTON (Map D)

44. Complex rectilinear cropmarks overlie the site of a neolithic interrupted ditch enclosure ("causewayed camp"), on a raised area of gravel between two streams. A small excavation in 1951-2 was reported to have disclosed a hearth and 4th century pottery. Pottery of 2nd to 4th century date was recovered during field-walking in December 1982. The area was known as "Stonyland Furlong" in 1794 (CRO map: W2/6/1-2). (See page 77).
> TL 0948.
> CUCAP; NMR AP; Johnston, 1956, 94 & 97; inf. J. Wood.
> SMR 585.

45. A large quantity of Roman pottery of the 2nd and 3rd centuries, including wasters, was turned up during construction of the Southern Feeder Gas Pipeline in 1976. Further finds were made in 1978, when the excavation of field drains uncovered part of a pottery kiln. (See page 40).
> TL 1044.
> Catherall et al., forthcoming; inf. Bedford Mus.
> SMR 9156.

46. A small group of rectilinear cropmarks adjacent to a stream. The lower half of a rotary quern of Hertfordshire puddingstone has been ploughed up in the same field.
> TL 0949.
> CUCAP; NMR AP; inf. author, 1975.
> SMR 586.

See also BEDFORD, G22.

CARLTON and CHELLINGTON (Map A)

47. A cropmark site has produced surface finds of dressed stone, roof and flue tile, and quantities of pottery, indicating the presence of a substantial building. (See pages 28 and 52).
> SP 9455.
> CUCAP; K. Field, *Northants. Archaeology* 8, Jun. 1973, 6.
> SMR 1781.

48. Iron Age and Roman pottery, located by field-walking.
> SP 9655.
> OS, 1976.
> SMR 5076.

49-51. Pottery scatters, located by field-walking.
> SP 9656.
> Inf. A.E. Brown, 1983.
> SMR 12130, 12139 & 12140.

52. Pottery scatter, located by field-walking.
> SP 9756.
> Inf. A.E. Brown, 1983.
> SMR 12141.

CHALGRAVE (Map F)

53. An intaglio ring showing Achilles with spear and helmet was found *c.* 1860 in the Old Brook, and later reached the hands of F.G. Gurney. It was near the point where a spring rises at the source of the brook, and may have been deposited as a votive object. (See page 56 and fig. 60).
> TL 0127.
> Gurney, 1920, 168; Martin Henig, "The Veneration of Heroes in the Roman army: the evidence of engraved Gemstones", *Brit.* 1, 1970, 249-265, esp. p. 254 & pl. xxiv, A & B.
> SMR 1419.

See also TODDINGTON, G261.

CHELLINGTON

See CARLTON and CHELLINGTON.

CLAPHAM (Map A)

54. A lead coffin was found when field drains were being dug, in or shortly before 1853. "An abundance of human remains" was found 100 yards (90 metres) away but may not have been related. (See page 47).
> TL 0253.
> *BAAS Notes* vol. 1, no. 2, May 1853, 21-23.
> SMR 1318.

CLIFTON (Map E)

55. Thomas Inskip of Shefford excavated a mound at Clifton in 1848. He found spurs, a knife and other metal objects, human bones and shells. Labourers had previously found a "red basin", which Inskip assumed to be a samian vessel. Fox recorded the existence of a Roman urn containing cremated bones in Cambridge Museum, labelled "from a barrow at

Clifton". These reports may be related, but identification as a Roman barrow must be treated with caution.

Unprov.

Thomas Inskip, *Journal of the British Archaeological Association* 4, 1849, 57-58; Fox, 1923, 197.

SMR 396.

CLOPHILL (Map D)

56. Pottery and building debris.
TL 1039.
Ampthill Arch. Soc., 1972.
SMR 2770.

COLMWORTH (Map B)

57. A 3rd century coin and Roman pottery. Trial excavations in 1940 by F.W. Kuhlicke produced no further evidence.
TL 1058.
Inf. Bedford Mus.
SMR 469.

58. Construction of the Southern Feeder Gas Pipeline in 1976 revealed a pit or ditch containing Roman pottery.
TL 1157.
Catherall *et al.*, forthcoming.
SMR 9831.

COPLE (Map D)

59. A group of enclosures, lying close to the River Ouse, was cut by a drainage scheme in 1978, producing pottery of the first half of the Roman period.
TL 0950.
CUCAP; NMR AP; inf. R. White.
SMR 1480.

See also WILLINGTON, G278.

CRANFIELD (Map C)

60. Pottery.
SP 9443.
Inf. Bedford Mus.
SMR 47.

61. A hoard of 4th century coins, deposited AD 348, was found in 1946. (See page 72).
SP 9443.
Philip V. Hill, "The Cranfield (Bedford) Hoard", *Num. Chron.* (6th series) 6, 1946, 159-162.
SMR 46.

62. Coins found in the churchyard during restoration of the church, *c*. 1845.
SP 9541.
BAAS Report 1, 1848, 6.
SMR 8321.

DUNSTABLE (Map F)

The meaning of Dunstable's Roman name, Durocobrivis (a preferable form to the more commonly quoted Durocobrivae) has long been the subject of debate, and is still very unclear. The two elements, *duro-* and *-brivae*, would normally be translated "fort" and "bridge" (as in Durobrivae at Water Newton near Peterborough). While the presence of a fort at or near Dunstable is a distinct possibility (see page 18), the complete absence of surface water precludes the existence of a bridge in the normal sense of the word. Nor can the middle syllable, *-co-*, be accommodated in this translation. In a recent discussion (Rivet and Smith, 1979, 349-350), based on detailed etymological analysis, 'portico-(of)-planks' is very tentatively put forward as a new suggestion, but clearly the question is still very open. (See page 30).

The Main Settlement

63. Friary Field was, until 1980, an open area in the south-west quadrant of Dunstable. Excavations by the Manshead Archaeological Society commenced in 1965, and while the first stage of the work was aimed at exploring the buildings of the Dominican Friory (founded in 1259), it soon became apparent that the site had a long history of Roman occupation. Roman finds were scattered throughout the surface layers and medieval features, and ditches and a well of Roman date appeared beneath the medieval levels. Subsequent excavations examined land further west.

Many finds from a variety of features (pits, ditches, wells, possible buildings) attest to the density of Roman occupation in this part of the town from the 1st to at least the 4th century. No substantial buildings have been located, though fragments of flue tile indicate that there may have been a hypocaust somewhere in the vicinity, probably destroyed by medieval and later building construction on the Watling Street frontage. There were several deep wells, one of which was excavated to a depth of 92 feet (28 metres), and contained pottery, bone, domestic and agricultural implements, and personal ornaments.

The most important discovery in Friary Field was a late Roman cemetery, only part of which was accessible for excavation. There was a central "formal" area, with ordered graves in rows, which was possibly first used in the 3rd century; this was surrounded on at least three sides by ditches, which began to be used for burials in the late 4th century. Some of the skeletons had been decapitated after death, which is a widespread, though little understood, Roman practice. Some were buried with grave goods ranging from hobnailed boots to collections of jewellery (necklaces, bracelets, finger-rings).

Decapitated burials, and burials with grave goods, occurred both in the formal cemetery area, and in the surrounding ditches, and the reason for the two different types of burial (formal and informal) is not clear. While it is possible that some sort of social distinction was in operation, this seems unlikely in view of the fact that one of the ditch burials, a young female, had perhaps the richest collection of jewellery from the cemetery. It may be that at the end of the 4th century the practice of burial in the ditches was adopted because of the comparative ease of excavating the graves in the ditch silt, perhaps beginning with the north ditch, where there are signs of coffin burials, and then utilising the south and east ditches, where burials seem to have been much more casual. Of a similar character are the burials in the tops of disused wells on the site, and the apparent deterioration of burial standards gives a very strong impression of a community under stress at the end of the Roman period.

Taken as a whole, the cemetery shows a normal proportion of different age groups, and of male and female burials, and gives no indication of a sudden end to the settlement, or massacre by incoming Saxons. Furthermore, the fact that some features on the site, such as drying ovens, appear to have been dug through the cemetery ditch, and therefore to post-date it, suggests that occupation may have continued into the early 5th century. (See pages 30, 34-5, 38, 42, 48-9, 51, 59-62 and 72-3, and fig. 23).

TL 0121.
Matthews and Hutchings, 1972; Mat-

thews *et al.*, 1981; see also *Manshead Mag.* vols. 16-21 (1966-1972) & 23-25 (1974-1979).
SMR 11284.

64. In 1964, redevelopment in Dunstable's north-east quadrant revealed traces of Roman occupation, which were investigated by the Manshead Archaeological Society. Several wells of Roman date were found, one of which had two human skeletons buried in its upper levels. Three areas marked by·depressions in the chalk, one associated with post-holes, were interpreted as primitive huts. A metalled roadway ran parallel to the Icknield Way, and 50 feet (15 metres) to the north of it, and probably served as a back lane for properties on the Icknield Way frontage. Finds from the site included pottery, animal bones, roof tile, iron implements, bronze ornaments, and glass and quern fragments. Coins gave a date range of 2nd to 4th century. (See pages 49 and 59).

TL 0121-0221.
Manshead Mag. 14, Dec. 1964, *passim.*
SMR 11270.

65. A well found beneath a cellar of a shop on the Watling Street was excavated by the Manshead Archaeological Society in 1963. It contained finds of both medieval and Roman date, with one medieval sherd at the lowest depth, and therefore was presumably dug in the medieval period. However, the quantity of Roman material shows that there must have been a considerable spread of Roman occupation debris on the ground in medieval times, which found its way into the well as it was back-filled.

TL 0121.
Manshead Mag. 12, Dec. 1963, 3-7.
SMR 11274.

66. A lead coffin and a skeleton, with Roman pottery, were found at the west end of Albion Street in the late 19th century. These may represent a burial area just outside the Roman settlement. (See page 47).

TL 0121.
Smith, 1894, 331.
SMR 122.

67. Roman pots were found *c.* 1960 during the building of an office block.

TL 0121.
Hagen, 1972, 36.
SMR 11275.

68, 69. Features identified as "refuse pits" by W.G. Smith were discovered during the execution of drainage works in 1901, in Cross Street and Chapel Alley (now Chapel Walk). Smith's description suggests these were actually ditches, probably boundary ditches which had been used for the dumping of domestic refuse — pottery, bones and oyster shells.

>TL 0121.
>Smith, 1904, 54.
>SMR 11276 & 11277.

70. Excavations by Manshead Archaeological Society in 1974-5 before development in St Mary's Street uncovered a cess pit, containing 2nd century pottery, bones and various fragments of domestic implements and ornaments, and a well which was in use until the 4th century.

>TL 0121.
>*Manshead Mag.* 24, Mar. 1975, 16-22.
>SMR 11273.

71. An electricity cable trench dug in 1970 near the Priory Church of St Peter uncovered a ditch with early Roman pottery.

>TL 0221.
>Hagen, 1972.
>SMR 11281.

Other sites and finds

72. Flint wall-footings, post-holes and Roman pottery were discovered during building operations in 1958, about 1 mile (1.6 km) southeast of the town centre.

>TL 0321.
>Bagshawe, 1959, 22 & fig. 1; Viatores, 1964, 61.
>SMR 1341.

73. Ditches and pottery were reported during the building of the Beecroft estate.

>TL 0022.
>Matthews, 1963, 60.
>SMR 1443.

74. Ditches producing early Roman pottery were uncovered during housing development in the 1960s.

>TL 0120.
>Inf. R. Hagen.
>SMR 762.

75. The northernmost barrow of the Five Knolls Bronze Age barrow cemetery, situated on a spur of the Chilterns overlooking the Icknield Way south-west of Dunstable, was excavated during the 1920s. More than 100 skeletons were found near the surface of the barrow, most of which probably derived from a medieval gallows on the site. Sherds of Roman pottery suggest that some of the remainder were of late Roman date. (See pages 61 and 72).

>TL 0021.
>G.C. Dunning and R.E.M. Wheeler, "A Barrow at Dunstable, Bedfordshire", *Arch. J.*

88, 1931, 193-217.
>SMR 138.

76. A small bow brooch with an attachment loop and decorated with cut-out triangles was found near Luton Road (fig. 34a).

>TL 0322.
>Inf. Luton Mus.
>SMR 12660.

77. Coins found on Gravel Pit Hill (originally in Houghton Regis, now in Dunstable parish).

>TL 0222.
>Brandreth, 1838, 103; Page and Keate, 1908, 8.
>SMR 127.

DUNTON (Map E)

78. 4th century pottery and tile.

>TL 2242.
>OS (J. Morris, 1958).
>SMR 521.

EASTCOTTS (Map D)

79. The construction of the Bedford Southern Orbital Sewer in 1977 exposed scatters of 1st and 2nd century pottery. The sewer pipe trench cut through a pottery kiln producing 2nd century grey ware in a similar tradition to the Mile Road kilns, Bedford (G15). (See page 40).

>TL 0747.
>White, 1980, 20-24.
>SMR 1623.

80. A report of kiln bars and wasters suggests a pottery kiln site.

>TL 0647.
>Inf. D.C. King, 1973.
>SMR 3640.

See also WILSTEAD, G281.

EGGINGTON (Map F)

81. F.G. Gurney recorded Roman grey ware "all over Eggington Hill", indicating occupation along the whole of the east-west ridge north of the modern village. Two areas of occupation (G82 & G83) have been examined in detail.

>SP 9525.
>CRO: X325/109-110 (Gurney notebook and diary, 1916-18).
>SMR 10730.

82. F.G. Gurney frequently visited the site of a sand pit on the ridge top at Manor Farm. His first main discovery was of an Iron Age inhumation burial, but he also observed Roman features, such as pits and ditches. The Manshead

Archaeological Society conducted some excavations in 1972, and some further Roman evidence was uncovered.

SP 9525.

CRO: X325, various Gurney notebooks, 1916-40; Frederick G. Gurney and C.F.C. Hawkes, "An Early Iron Age Inhumation-Burial at Egginton, Bedfordshire", *Ant. J.* 20, 1940, 230-244; *Manshead Mag.* 22, 1973, 3-17.

SMR 9.

83. F.G. Gurney identified a major concentration of Roman pottery at Charity Farm on the west end of the ridge. Excavations by the Manshead Archaeological Society in 1959 and 1962 produced evidence of Roman ditches and depressions of Roman date, possibly hut sites. The pottery gave a date range of 2nd to 4th century.

SP 9425-9525.

CRO: X325, various Gurney notebooks, 1916-18; *Manshead Mag.* 6, Jun. 1961, 75-84; 7, Nov. 1961, 86; 9, Aug. 1962, 142-143.

SMR 1437.

84. "Indications of Romano-British finds."

SP 9625.

F.G. Gurney map in Luton Mus., acc. no. 5/50/60.

SMR 12747.

ELSTOW (Map D)

85. Excavations on the site of Elstow Abbey, 1965-1972, produced some evidence of 1st to 4th century Roman occupation, in the form of a scatter of features below the medieval levels, with some pottery and coins.

TL 0447.

David Baker, *Beds. Arch. J.* 3, 1966, 23-24; *Beds. Arch. J.* 4, 1969, 27-28.

SMR 262.

86. Cropmarks were investigated by P.J. Woodward in 1976 before the construction of the Bedford Southern Orbital Sewer. They were mostly of Iron Age and medieval origin, but a few ditches and gullies could be attributed to occupation in the Roman period.

TL 0547.

CUCAP; P.J. Woodward, "Excavations at Pear Tree Farm, Elstow, Bedfordshire, 1976", *Beds. Arch. J.* 12, 1977, 27-54.

SMR 1624.

87. 3rd to 4th century pottery with stone, roof-tiles, and fragments of daub found in 1936. (See page 53n83).

TL 0446.

Inf. Bedford Mus.

SMR 263.

88. The construction of the Bedford Southern Orbital Sewer in 1977 uncovered a number of small features, mostly pits and gullies, producing Roman pottery.

TL 0547.

White, 1980, 19.

SMR 8356.

EYEWORTH (Map E)

89. A villa site has been located through finds brought up by the plough. Building material, wall-plaster, and mosaic fragments indicate a substantial building of fairly high standard. Pottery and coins of 2nd to 3rd century date have also been found.

TL 2545.

OS, 1974; *Beds. Arch. J.* 8, 1973, 143.

SMR 517.

FELMERSHAM (Map A)

90. In 1972, a watching-brief and rescue excavations in advance of gravel extraction recovered evidence of a late Roman farmstead east of Radwell. Two timber buildings lay at the edge of a network of rectangular fields. Roof and flue tile and fragments of window glass suggest that a substantial building may be located outside the quarried area. The pottery and coins give a date range of 3rd to 4th century. Evidence of iron smelting. (See pages 27, 38n16, 48 and 51).

TL 0157.

Hall, 1973.

SMR 1797.

91. Early Roman pottery, with evidence of occupation, located by field-walking.

SP 9856.

Hall and Hutchings, 1972, 9.

SMR 2646.

92. Pottery, with evidence of occupation, located by field-walking.

SP 9757.

Hall and Hutchings, 1972, 9.

SMR 2647.

93. Pottery scatter, located by field-walking.

SP 9856.

Hall and Hutchings, 1972, 9.

SMR 2648.

FLITTON (Map D)

94. Cremation in urns, found in 1823, may have come from a Belgic or Roman cemetery.

Unprov.

Page and Keate, 1908, 7.
SMR 216.

95. A scatter of tile and 3rd to 4th century pottery, located by field-walking.

TL 0433.
Fadden, 1975, 2-4.
SMR 3642.

96. Some pottery was found during excavations for a pipeline at Greenfield, and donated to Bedford Museum in 1965. A water main runs north from Greenfield through the large site near Ruxox (see MAULDEN G174), from where these finds may therefore have come. (See figs. 29a and 31).

c. TL 0535.
Inf. Bedford Mus.
SMR 112.

FLITWICK (Map C)

97. A square cropmark, in an area scheduled for housing development, was investigated in 1973-4 by the Ampthill and District Archaeological Society. The enclosure itself appears to have been dug in the 2nd century, and in the centre was a T-shaped drying oven. No other occupation evidence was identified, though the interior of the enclosure was not stripped. The site has now been developed. (See pages 25, 33 and 52).

TL 0235.
Kevan Fadden, "The Excavation of a Roman Corn-Drying Oven at Manor Way, Flitwick", *Beds. Arch. J.* 11, 1976, 23-24.
SMR 564.

98. A hoard of 177 coins of Tetricus II (AD 268-273) was found during agricultural drainage works at Priestley Farm in 1880. (See page 72).

TL 0233.
Maj. W. Cooper Cooper, *PSA* (2nd series) 8, 1879-81, 271-273; Page and Keate, 1908, 7.
SMR 226.

See MAULDEN, G174, for Roman occupation at Ruxox Farm.

GRAVENHURST (Map D)

99. An agricultural drainage trench dug in 1978 cut through a ditch containing ashes and early Roman pottery.

TL 1035.
Inf. Luton Mus.
SMR 11291.

GREAT BARFORD (Map B)

100. A rectangular cropmark enclosure has not produced any dating evidence, but is likely to be of Roman origin. The regularity of its layout suggests it may be centred round a substantial building.

TL 1251.
CUCAP.
SMR 596.

101. Road improvement works in 1969 uncovered pits and ditches which produced 1st and 2nd century Roman pottery, burnt building material, and a human skeleton. Cropmarks of enclosures have been recorded in an adjacent area.

TL 1453.
CUCAP; G. Rudd in Taylor and Woodward, 1982 forthcoming.
SMR 482.

102. Cropmarks of enclosures and a trackway have produced a few sherds of Roman pottery.

TL 1153.
CUCAP; OS, 1975.
SMR 1630.

103. The Southern Feeder Gas Pipeline, constructed in 1976, revealed two features containing Roman pottery.

TL 1152.
Catherall *et al.*, forthcoming.
SMR 9833.

HARROLD (Map A)

104. 19th century reports of quantities of coins and an oculist's stamp from "a farm just outside Harrold" refer to Lodge Farm, on a slope overlooking the Ouse. The site was rediscovered in 1968 by P. and D. Panter in the form of a large spread of building material and pottery. Excavations revealed pottery kilns which have been extensively examined by A.E. Brown, demonstrating pottery and tile production in a shell-tempered ware from the 1st to the 4th century. (See pages 39, 43, 49 and 53-4, and fig. 53).

SP 9335.
Steward, 1898, 2-15; Page and Keate, 1908, 8; *Wolverton and District Archaeological Society Journal*, 2, 1969, 10 & 16; A.E. Brown, "Excavations at Harrold, Bedfordshire, 1969", *Wolverton Historical Journal*, 1970, 16-18; Brown, 1972; *Brit.* 1, 1970, 288; 2, 1971, 267; 3, 1972, 327.
SMR 1182.

105. Roman vessels were reported from a gravel pit in 1814-15, in a field called Potter's Close, some containing cremated remains. Of the two vessels recorded one is a 1st century two-handled flagon (see Title Page), another is a jar of Belgic type. Two skeletons were also reported. These finds probably represent the site of a cemetery of the late Belgic or early Roman period.

> SP 9456.
> CRO: Longuet-Higgins scrapbook, p. 29 (mic. 84); interleaved copy of Lysons and Lysons, 1813 edition, opposite p. 91; BC 529, 534-536, Thomas Orlebar Marsh papers.
> SMR 60.

106. A scatter of tile and pottery (including samian ware), located by field-walking. A report by the farmer of herringbone walling suggests the footings of a stone building.

> SP 9458.
> OS, 1974.
> SMR 6379.

107. Pottery with evidence of occupation, located by field-walking.

> SP 9259.
> Hall and Nickerson, 1966, 5.
> SMR 840.

108. Pottery and iron slag, located by field-walking.

> SP 9358.
> Hall and Nickerson, 1966, 5.
> SMR 838.

109. Pottery with evidence of occupation, located by field-walking.

> SP 9257.
> Hall and Nickerson, 1966, 5.
> SMR 842.

110. Pottery, with iron slag and pebbles, located by field-walking.

> SP 9156.
> Hall and Nickerson, 1966, 5.
> SMR 832.

111. Pottery scatter, located by field-walking.

> SP 9156.
> Hall and Nickerson, 1966, 5.
> SMR 830.

112. Pottery, stone and tile, located by field-walking.

> SP 9255.
> Hall and Nickerson, 1966, 5 (published grid reference amended by D. Hall, personal communication).
> SMR 4428.

HAYNES (Map D)

113. Scatter of early Roman pottery.

> TL 1041.
> Inf. R. Hagen, 1983.
> SMR 3468.

HEATH & REACH (Map F)

114. The Double Arches Sandpit, Overendgreen, has produced much Roman material since it was opened in 1915. F.G. Gurney recorded "Roman potsherds in great quantities", and two skeletons, one of which showed severe wounds to the skull. In the 1950s, Roman pits and further pottery were discovered, and regular visits by J.A. Griffin led to the identification of a stone-lined well. The machine driver also reported the destruction of a stone floor in the same area. The quantity and nature of these finds (which were made when boulder clay and gault clay were stripped off to reach the sand underneath) indicate intensive Roman occupation, possibly associated with a substantial building or villa. (See page 29).

> SP 9239.
> CRO: X325/114, Gurney notebook, 1920-1; *Leighton Buzzard Observer*, 3 & 10 Mar. 1931; *Manshead Mag.* 1, Oct. 1958, 9; J.A. Griffin, "Roman Site and Well, Double Arches Sand Pit, Leighton Buzzard", *Manshead Mag.* 20, Spring 1970, 25-31; Richard Hagen, "A second century Roman well near Leighton Buzzard", *Beds. Arch. J.* 6, 1971, 71-72.
> SMR 1170.

115. 2 pots excavated from a sandpit in 1927.

> SP 9327.
> Richmond, 1928, 110.
> SMR 6.

HIGHAM GOBION (Map G)

116. A settlement site somewhere in the parish is indicated by finds made in the 19th century, including "coins, cinerary urns and an amphora".

> Unprov.
> Watkin, 1882, 281-282; Page and Keate, 1908, 8.
> SMR 411.

HOCKLIFFE (Map F)

117. Pottery.

> SP 9725.
> F.G. Gurney map in Luton Mus., acc. no. 6/50/60.
> SMR 1376.

HOUGHTON CONQUEST (Map C)

118. Pottery scatter, located by field-walking.

> TL 0340.
> Fadden, 1975, 2-3.
> SMR 2425.

HOUGHTON REGIS (Map F)

119. On Puddlehill, a long sequence of prehistoric occupation was followed by Roman settlement over much of the hilltop, lasting throughout the Roman period. Excavations by the Manshead Archaeological Society from 1951 to 1975 recovered information on pits, ditches, post-holes and possible hut sites, both on top of the hill, and on lower ground on its southern slopes. A quarry worker reported the destruction of the foundations of a substantial building.

A bronze pin (fig. 36a), which W.G. Smith found after it had fallen from a pit on the top of the Watling Street cutting at Puddlehill, suggests that Roman occupation extended along the hill top as far west as the Roman road.

TL 0023-0123.

Page and Keate, 1908, 7; Matthews, 1963, 55-61; *Manshead Mag.* 1, Oct. 1958, 8; 3, Jul. 1959, 25 & 30; 4, Jun. 1960, 43-45; 13, Oct. 1964, 3-25.

SMR 687.

120. In the area of the Iron Age hillfort of Maiden Bower, Roman finds, especially coins, have been recorded for several centuries. In 1907, W.G. Smith recovered pottery, including samian, from cremation burials which were destroyed by quarrying to the north-west. He also reported quern fragments of Andernach lava (see page 34n4) and Hertfordshire puddingstone, pieces of glass and an intaglio ring. A toilet implement set, consisting of tweezers and a toothpick or nail-cleaner, was found nearby in 1917 (fig. 36b).

SP 9922.

Worthington G. Smith, *PSA* (2nd series) 27, 1914-15, 148-150; Page and Keate, 1908, 9; inf. Luton Mus.

SMR 666.

121. In 1829, a well was discovered during the excavation of a cutting for the Dunstable-Leighton Buzzard railway line, north of Maiden Bower, and recorded by J. Wyatt and W. Monkhouse. It was at least 120 feet (36 metres) deep, and was filled with a variety of Roman material, including pottery, tile, shaped stones, human and animal bones, burnt wood and ashes. The contents of the well suggest that a fairly substantial building may have been demolished and the debris thrown down the well after it had gone out of use. (See pages 58-9).

SP 9922.

Monkhouse, 1860, 281-283.

SMR 22.

See also DUNSTABLE, G77.

HULCOTE AND SALFORD (Map C)

122. Some poorly defined cropmarks north-west of Salford have not been dated, but a field system immediately to the west in Buckinghamshire, excavated in advance of gravel extraction, proved to date from the 2nd century onwards.

SP 9240.

Hunting Surveys Ltd AP; M.R. Petchey, "A Roman Field System at Broughton, Buckinghamshire", *Records of Bucks.* 20, pt. 4, 1978, 637-645.

SMR 7721.

HYDE (Map G)

123. A large coin hoard (possibly numbering about 1000 coins) was unearthed during landscaping works in 1862 on the Luton Hoo estate. Many were dispersed among workmen, but those that were traced and identified give a deposition date of *c.* AD 270.

TL 1018.

John Evans, "Account of a hoard of Roman coins found near Luton, Bedfordshire", *Num. Chron.* n.s.10, Jun. 1863, 112-118 (reprinted in *BAAS Notes* vol. 1, no. 13, Mar. 1864, 193-198; Watkin, 1882, 288; J.F. Drinkwater, "Coin-Hoards and the Chronology of the Gallic Emperors", *Brit.* 5, 1974, 289-292, esp. pp. 298-299.

SMR 352.

124. A bronze mount decorated with a hound and stag; found at New Mill End by E. Bradley. (See page 47 and fig. 42).

*c.*TL 1218.

Inf. Luton Mus.

SMR 1592.

KEMPSTON (Map C)

125. The gravel plateau on which the centre of modern Kempston lies was extensively exploited for gravel in the 19th century. Many finds of all periods were recovered by workmen, some of which were recorded by local antiquaries. An extensive Belgic and early Roman cemetery was found, probably centred round a Bronze Age barrow or barrow cemetery. (See pages 42, 56, 60 and 73, and figs. 28c, 29b & c, 32 and 57).

TL 0247-0347.

T.G. Elger, *Beds. Mercury*, 8 Mar. 1890, p. 3; T.G. Elger, *PSA* (2nd series) 13, 1889-91, 240-242; Langdon, 1925, 50-53, pl.12.

SMR 256.

126. A hoard of silver coins, deposited *c.*AD 395, was discovered during house building on the Hillgrounds estate in 1976. (See pages 72-3).

TL 0248.
Inf. Bedford Mus.
SMR 1191.

KEMPSTON RURAL (Map C)

127. In 1937, F.W. Kuhlicke investigated the site of a Roman building at Moor End, with the Bedford Modern School Field Club. The discovery of stone footings, roof and floor tiles, and tesserae implies a substantial building or villa. The pottery and coins gave a date range of 2nd to 4th century.

TL 0050.
Bedford Modern School Field Club Journal and Museum Bulletin 4, Nov. 1937, 90 (Anon. but almost certainly F.W. Kuhlicke); inf. Bedford Mus.
SMR 245.

128. Considerable quantities of pottery, coins and a bronze figurine have been found at Church End. A coin hoard found in the vicinity may be related. (See pages 45 and 72-3).

TL 0147.
CRO: X69/16, *BAAS Minute Book*, p. 110 (11 Nov. 1851), p. 125 (21 Sep. 1852); C.R. Parrott, *All Saints Parish Church, Kempston: A History*, 1979, 79; inf. Bedford Mus.
SMR 162.

129. A pit containing early Roman pottery was uncovered during agricultural drainage operations in 1972.

TL 0047.
Beds. Arch. J. 7, 1972, 92-93.
SMR 977.

KENSWORTH (Map F)

130. Roman pottery from Kensworth churchyard.

TL 0319.
Smith, 1904, 52.
SMR 106.

131. A section dug across the supposed line of Watling Street (see page 63) produced a bronze pin and a small Roman sherd.

TL 0419.
Viatores, 1964, 30-31 (R.W. Bagshawe.
SMR 5146.

See WHIPSNADE, G277 for Roman finds from Kensworth Common.

KNOTTING AND SOULDROP (Map A)

132. A spread of 1st to 3rd century pottery,

kiln bars, grey ware pottery wasters, querns and roof tiles indicate a pottery production site: located by field-walking.

SP 9862.
Hall and Hutchings, 1972, 11.
SMR 2719.

133. Pottery, with evidence of occupation, located by field-walking.

SP 9762.
Hall and Hutchings, 1972, 10.
SMR 2720.

134. Pottery scatter, located by field-walking.

SP 9963.
Inf. M. Booth, 1983.
SMR 1965.

135. Pottery scatter, located by field-walking.

TL 0063.
Inf. M. Booth, 1976.
SMR 828.

136. An area of occupation, with building debris, tile and pottery, located by field-walking.

TL 0063.
Inf. M. Booth, 1976.
SMR 392.

137. A large area of Roman finds and iron slag patches, located by field-walking.

TL 0063.
Hall and Hutchings, 1972, 10; inf. M. Booth, 1976.
SMR 2663.

138. Pottery, with evidence of occupation, located by field-walking.

TL 0063.
Hall and Hutchings, 1972, 10.
SMR 2659.

139. Pottery scatter, including colour-coated ware, located by field-walking.

TL 0063.
Inf. M. Booth, 1983.
SMR 6665.

140. Pottery scatter, located by field-walking.

TL 0163.
Inf. M. Booth, 1983.
SMR 1966.

141. A few sherds, located by field-walking.

TL 0163.
Hall and Hutchings, 1972, 10.
SMR 2661.

142. Pottery scatter, located by field-walking.

TL 0061.
Inf. M. Booth, 1983.
SMR 1969.

143. An area of occupation covering 10 acres, located by field-walking.

TL 0061.
Hall and Hutchings, 1972, 10.

SMR 2658.

144. Pottery scatter, located by field-walking.

TL 0161.

Inf. M. Booth, 1983.

SMR 2693.

145. Early Roman pottery, with evidence of occupation, located by field-walking.

TL 0161.

Hall and Hutchings, 1972, 10.

SMR 2657.

LANGFORD (Map E)

146. Scatter of pottery, including samian ware, and roof tile, located by field-walking.

TL 2039.

Inf. D.C. King.

SMR 2796.

LEIGHTON-LINSLADE (Map F)

147. F.G. Gurney recorded Roman pottery and "a fine shark's tooth" from a gravel pit at Tiddingford Hill, where "three or four sepulchral urns" had been found in 1854. (See page 59).

SP 9123.

James Joseph Sheahan, *History and Topography of Buckinghamshire*, 1862, 705; Gurney documents, 1919 and 1938, Bucks. Arch. Soc., Aylesbury.

SMR 10725.

148. The base of a "burial urn with ashes . . . of Castor ware and a local imitation", was found at Rackley Holes, Grovebury.

SP 9123.

Richmond, 1928, 110.

SMR 10728.

149. F.G. Gurney recorded a Roman pit with pottery from sandpits at Grovebury.

SP 9123.

Gurney notebook, 1919, Bucks. Arch. Soc., Aylesbury; CRO: X325/160, Gurney notebook, 1918-20.

SMR 10727.

150. A well, lined with sandstone and said at the time to be Roman, was found in Page's Park, Leighton Buzzard, though no datable finds were reported. (See page 52).

SP 9224.

Smith, 1894, 328; Page and Keate, 1908, 8.

SMR 20.

151. Pottery, found 1961.

SP 9124.

Bucks. County Mus.(Bucks. SMR no. 1464).

SMR 819.

152. 1st and 2nd century coins from Leighton Buzzard churchyard.

SP 9124.

Richmond; 1928, 110.

SMR 9659.

LIDLINGTON (Map C)

153. Pottery scatter; mostly very coarse wares, with a few samian sherds.

SP 9839.

Inf. A. Davies, 1983.

SMR 1594.

Limbury

See LUTON, G154.

Linslade

See LEIGHTON-LINSLADE.

LUTON (Map G)

154. In the early 20th century, W.G. Smith and F.G. Gurney recorded Roman occupation debris and human skeletons from a gravel pit on Stoney Hill at Limbury. In 1953, rescue excavations by W.H. Manning during housing development identified many Roman features including ditches, pits, cobbled floors, hearths and post-holes. Among the finds were large quantities of pottery, iron, bronze and bone objects, glass and lead fragments, coins, personal ornaments and domestic utensils. The dating evidence of the coins and pottery suggests an expansion and intensification of settlement in the 3rd and 4th centuries. Further work by R. Lawson in 1957 uncovered 15 burials, evidence of bronze-working, and the metalling of a road running parallel to the Icknield Way. In subsequent years, many individual finds, especially coins, have been reported by the residents of the new estate.

The excavation evidence and other finds recorded suggest that an extensive settlement grew up along the line of the Icknield Way north of the River Lea. This may have been centred round a villa, as a possible mosaic was reported to have been found during building work in 1928. (See pages 28, 31, 35, 38, 40-1, 43, 48, 53-4 and 73, and figs. 21, 37a and 46a).

TL 0724.

W.G. Smith, *PSA* (2nd series) 21, 1906-7, 82-83; Page and Keate, 1908, 8; CRO: X325, various Gurney notebooks, 1914-18; Austin, 1928, 23; Manning, 1955, 21-27; *JRS* 47, 1957, 214; Dyer and Dony, 1975, 15.

SMR 115.

155. Roman floor and flue tiles were reported to have been ploughed up on Farley Farm in 1911, though the existence of a substantial building or villa has not been confirmed.

TL 0721.

Austin, 1928, 25.

SMR 204.

156. In 1882, south of Waulud's Bank, two skeletons were found, with large quantities of pottery and some "clay bars" which appear to have been from a pottery kiln. (See page 40).

TL 0624.

Maj. W. Cooper Cooper, PSA (2nd series) 10, 1883-5, 133-135; Page and Keate, 1908, 8; Austin, 1928, 16.

SMR 166.

157. 1st century pottery and a brooch from Toddington Road found in 1962.

TL 0524.

Inf. Luton Mus.

SMR 2837.

158. Roman coins have been found in the area of the prehistoric site known as Waulud's Bank. A few sherds of Belgic and Roman pottery were noted during excavation of the site by J. Dyer in 1953. About 1970 a water main was laid for nearly 200 metres (650 feet) along the centre of the earthwork ditch on its northern side. About 1 metre (3 feet) from the surface, a thick scatter of Roman pottery (probably 3rd century) and animal bone was uncovered. Reports from the building of the adjoining flats, of pottery and bone, confirm the presence of occupational debris in this area, though no building foundations were observed.

TL 0624.

Davis, 1855, 39; James F. Dyer, "A Secondary Neolithic Camp at Waulud's Bank, Leagrave", Beds. Arch. J. 2, 1964, 1-15, esp. 5; inf. J. Dyer, 1983.

SMR 820.

159. South of the River Lea at Leagrave, and close to the point where it was forded by the Icknield Way, excavations during housing development in 1953 uncovered occupation of the later Iron Age and early Roman periods.

TL 0624.

James F. Dyer, "Willow Way Marsh Site, Leagrave, Bedfordshire", Beds. Archaeologist 1, 1955-6, 56-58.

SMR 167.

160. House construction at Rosslyn Crescent in 1962 revealed a small Belgic cemetery, and early Roman occupation. Earlier this century, Roman occupation was recorded by F.G. Gurney from a gravel pit known as "Biscot Grange Pit" in the area immediately to the west.

TL 0824.

CRO: X325, various Gurney notebooks, 1914-18; Manshead Mag. 11, Apr. 1963, 3-10.

SMR 1946.

161. A scatter of probably late 3rd and early 4th century pottery, with scraps of burnt bone and charcoal.

TL 0924.

Inf. J. Dyer, 1981.

SMR 698.

162. "Much broken pottery, with Roman and British coins" were found during drainage works in the early 19th century, near Stockingstone Lane.

TL 0823.

Austin, 1928, 23.

SMR 203.

163. When the New Bedford Road (opened in 1832) was being constructed, workmen dug out "several earthen jars . . . a quantity of broken pieces, made of coarse red earth . . . a large quantity of oyster shells buried in holes about three feet [1 metre] deep". Austin identified these finds as Roman.

TL 0823.

Davis, 1855, 46; Austin, 1928, 23.

SMR 206.

164. 1st century pottery and a brooch were found with cremation burials in 1926, during house-building on Richmond Hill. One of the cremations was associated with a number of bird bones (see page 38).

TL 0922.

Austin, 1928, 28-29; inf. Luton Mus.

SMR 183.

165. A Roman storage jar was exposed in the section of a new road at Round Green in 1921. Skeletons were also reported from the area.

TL 1022.

Austin, 1928, 26.

SMR 359.

166. Pottery found in Stopsley Brickyard, c. 1938.

TL 1023.

Inf. Luton Mus.

SMR 11297.

167. A pit containing 2nd century pottery was observed in a house foundation trench in Bradley Road, in 1970.

TL 0522.

Inf. Luton Mus.

SMR 2846.

168. Pottery from Rothesay Road cemetery.

TL 0821.

Inf. Luton Mus.

SMR 1981.

169. Roman pottery was found at Brache Farm in 1858, and a coin of Constantine I (AD 306-337) from the same area was donated to Luton Museum in 1940.

TL 0920.

Austin, 1928, 24; inf. Luton Mus.

SMR 1980.

170. A ditch containing Roman pottery was revealed when an electricity sub-station and lighting control centre were constructed at Luton Airport in 1960.

TL 1121.

Inf. Luton Mus.

SMR 1466.

171. Excavations by J. Dyer on the Iron Age linear earthworks known as Dray's Ditches have demonstrated that by the Roman period the ditches, previously unbroken, had silted sufficiently for the Icknield Way to cross them. In the ruts were pieces of iron horse- and ox-shoes and coins of Vespasian (AD 69-79) and Tetricus I (AD 271-273).

TL 0826.

Brit. 3, 1972, 237; *Beds. Arch. J.* 6, 1971, 87-88.

SMR 113.

172. Coins found at the Corporation Nursery Ground, Stockwood Park, included some of Tetricus I (AD 271-273) and a number which were identified as being of 4th century date.

TL 0819.

Inf. Luton Mus.

SMR 10471.

MARSTON MORETAINE (Map C)

173. Scatter of pottery, including samian, located by field-walking.

SP 9742.

Inf. A. Davies, 1984.

SMR 12476.

MAULDEN (Map D)

174. Near to Ruxox Farm, Flitwick, is an extensive area of Roman occupation. The site was first investigated by T.H.Gardner in the 1950s, who identified concentrations of Roman pottery in the ploughsoil, and cut a number of small trial trenches in various locations. The pottery and coins recovered gave a range of dates throughout the Roman period. Some of the finds lay in waterlogged land near the river, demonstrating how climatic deterioration from

the end of the Roman period led to a rise in the water level, and the formation of peat deposits which are a feature of the Flit valley in this area. Gardner located several scatters of stone, but did not recover any building plans.

More recent work by the Ampthill and District Archaeological Society has confirmed the richness of the occupation, with finds of pins, brooches, intaglios, painted wall-plaster, tesserae and pipeclay figurines having been reported. There is a strong possibility that these derive from a temple site at the centre of the settlement, though there may also have been a villa in the area. (See pages 28, 31-2, 35, 48, 56, 59 and 74, and figs. 24c, 35c & d, 47a, 54 and 55). (See also Flitton, G96).

TL 0436-0536.

CRO: CRT/Flitwick/1 (notes by T.H. Gardner 1957-1961; Viatores, 1964, 285 & 289-290; *Beds. Arch. J.* 4, 1969, 86; 5, 1970, 124; 6, 1971, 87; 7, 1972, 93; 8, 1973, 141; *CBA Gp. 9 NL* 2, 1972, 20; Ampthill Arch. Soc., 1973, 2-4; inf. Ampthill Arch. Soc.; see also Kevan Fadden, "Ruxox Farm, Maulden: 1. The Prehistoric Finds", *Beds. Arch. J.* 5, 1970, 1-4, esp. p.3.

SMR 918.

175. An amphora was found *c*.1798 in the peat on Maulden Moor "with several urns . . . containing bones and ashes, and fragments of the red pottery enriched with figures and other ornaments". This description sounds like a Belgic "wealthy" burial, with imported samian pottery. Maulden Moor lies adjacent to the area covered by G174, to which this find may be related. (See pages 8 and 28).

c.TL 0536.

Lysons and Lysons, 1806, 24.

SMR 223.

176. Pottery scatter, located by field-walking.

TL 0639.

Inf. Ampthill Arch. Soc.

SMR 9810.

MELCHBOURNE and YIELDEN (Map A)

177. A site revealed when pottery, tesserae and building stones were ploughed up in the 19th century was investigated by Rev. R.S. Baker in 1881. He found the "merest fragments of foundations", but it is likely that a substantial building or villa once existed on the site. Deep steam ploughing had been employed in the 19th century, probably destroying most of the building foundations, though the site may have been re-located by field-walking in recent years.

TL 0067.

Rev. R.S. Baker, *AASRP* 16, pt. 2, 1882, 263; Hall and Hutchings, 1972, 12.

SMR 340.

MILTON ERNEST (Map A)

178. An extensive pottery scatter, with iron slag, located by field-walking. Excavations by North Bedfordshire Archaeological Society at the adjacent medieval moated site of Yarlswood also recovered evidence of Roman occupation.

TL 0356.

Hutchings, 1969, 76; *Beds. Mag.* 9, 1963-5, 302.

SMR 6749.

179. Occupation site, located by field-walking.

TL 0056.

Hutchings, 1969, 75.

SMR 906.

180. Dense scatter of pottery.

TL 0155.

Inf. P. Dempster.

SMR 1937.

Newnham

See Bedford, G13.

NORTHILL (Map D)

181. In 1845, during the excavation of field drains, two skeletons were found in Northill, associated with three glass vessels, some samian fragments, and an iron object interpreted as a bracket for hanging a lamp. Two glass vessels are preserved in Bedford Museum. (See pages 51 and fig. 49a).

TL 1445.

Gent's. Mag. n.s. 24, 1845, 64; Page and Keate, 1908, 9; Kennett, 1970, 203.

SMR 425.

182. Animal bones and 4th century pottery were found in Home Wood in 1949.

TL 1446.

OS, 1953.

SMR 430.

183. Roman pottery has been reported from the vicinity of Upper Caldecote, and a pit containing Roman pottery was uncovered in recent years in the same area.

*c.*TL 1645.

Page and Keate, 1908, 9; inf. D.H. Kennett, 1971.

SMR 454 & 978.

OAKLEY (Map A)

184. Roman coins from Trajan (AD 97-117) onwards, and some later Roman pottery, found near Oakley Bridge; located during field-walking by P.G. Tilson.

TL 0053.

Beds. Arch. J. 7, 1972, 94.

SMR 7683.

185. Dredging near Stafford Bridge in 1971-2 produced some Roman pottery, with a loom-weight and quern fragment which may have been Roman; finds reported by A. East.

TL 0054.

Beds. Arch. J. 7, 1972, 94.

SMR 7684.

ODELL (Map A)

186. A Roman site known from surface scatters has produced pottery, roof and flue tile and dressed building stone, and may be a villa. The coins and pottery are mainly 3rd to 4th century. (See page 52).

SP 9759.

Hall and Hutchings, 1972, 10; inf. G.J. Dring, 1980.

SMR 2669.

187. A Belgic and Roman farmstead site was excavated by Brian Dix in advance of gravel extraction, in 1974-8. It was established at the end of the 1st century BC, when a field system was laid out based on a small living enclosure, containing two circular timber-built houses. Immediately outside this living enclosure were two small cremation cemeteries in use in the second quarter of the 1st century AD.

There was no immediate change in the character of the settlement at the Roman Conquest, but at the end of the 1st century the homestead site was relocated. Circular houses were constructed at first, but these were eventually replaced by a rectangular timber building which continued in use probably until the mid-4th century. Associated with these structures were other features typical of Roman rural settlements, such as stone-lined wells and a drying kiln. Throughout the centuries of occupation the field system continued in use with frequent maintenance and occasional internal alteration. (See pages 14, 24-5, 33, 36n12, 38, 45, 58, 61 and 68, and figs. 9, 10, 19 and 49b).

SP 9556.

CUCAP; Brian Dix, "Odell: A River Valley Farm", *Current Archaeology* 66, Apr. 1979, 215-218; Brian Dix, "Excavations at Harrold Pit, Odell, 1974-1978: A Preliminary Report", *Beds. Arch. J.* 14, 1980, 15-18; Dix, 1983 forthcoming.

SMR 543.

188. Occupation, with pottery and a few roof tiles, covering about one acre; located by field-walking.

SP 9558.
Hall and Hutchings, 1972, 10.
SMR 2673.

189. Occupation, with some iron slag, covering about one acre; located by field-walking.

SP 9658.
Hall and Hutchings, 1972, 10.
SMR 2675.

190. Pottery scatter, located by field-walking.

SP 9758.
Hall and Hutchings, 1972, 10.
SMR 2678.

OLD WARDEN (Map D)

191. Two imported amphorae were found on Quints Hill, some time before 1845. Subsequent excavations by Thomas Inskip uncovered two lathe-turned vases of Kimmeridge shale, and hoops of iron (probably the remains of an iron-bound wooden bucket) which enclosed a cremation. The finds probably date from the eve of the Roman conquest. (See pages 15, 28, and 51).

TL 1344.
Dryden, 1845, 20; Fox, 1923, 96 & 98-99.
SMR 459.

PAVENHAM (Map A)

192. A regular rectangular enclosure has been identified from cropmarks. Some Roman pottery has been found, and it may be the site of a villa or substantial building, though aerial photographs show no sign of internal structures. (See page 28 and fig. 16).

TL 0155.
CUCAP; OS, 1977.
SMR 1819.

193. Bronze figurine.

Unprov.
OS (F.W. Kuhlicke, 1950).
SMR 69.

PODINGTON (Map A)

194. Pottery scatter, located by field-walking.
SP 9363.
Hall and Nickerson, 1966, 5.
SMR 849.

195. Pottery scatter, located by field-walking.
SP 9463.
Hall and Nickerson, 1966, 5.

SMR 850.

196. Occupation, with building stone and roof tile, located by field-walking.

SP 9363.
Hall and Hutchings, 1972, 9.
SMR 2650.

197. Occupation, with building stone and tile, located by field-walking.

SP 9362.
Hall and Nickerson, 1966, 5.
SMR 848.

198. A few Roman sherds, located by field-walking.

SP 9463.
Hall and Hutchings, 1972, 10.
SMR 2680.

199. Pottery and occupation, covering about one acre, located by field-walking.

SP 9462.
Hall and Hutchings, 1972, 10.
SMR 2681.

200. Occupation, with pottery and pebbles, located by field-walking.

SP 9662.
Hall and Hutchings, 1972, 10.
SMR 1331.

201. c.1840, a bronze figure of a soldier was ploughed up in a field near Hinwick, known as Bellum or Bellams. It is said to have come from the same field in which 3rd and 4th century pottery and building debris have been recovered more recently through field-walking. (See page 45).

SP 9461.
VCH Beds. 3, 1912, 82; BNFAS 4, Apr. 1970, 12; Beds. Arch. J. 6, 1971, 87; Hall and Hutchings, 1972, 10.
SMR 2654.

202. Finds made on Podington Wold in the early 19th century included a hoard of 15 coins in a pot, coins of Gallienus (AD 253-268) and Philippus Augustus (AD 244-249), a stone described as of circular form with a hole for a winch, which sounds like a rotary quern, and fragments of pottery. (See page 72).

c.SP 9562-9662.
CRO: BC 512/12, Thomas Orlebar Marsh papers, 1817.
SMR 11306.

POTTON (Map E)

203. In an area of rather indeterminate cropmarks, sand extraction in 1980 exposed a ditch containing 1st and 2nd century pottery.

TL 2250.
NMR AP; inf. R.F. White.
SMR 658.

Puddlehill
See HOUGHTON REGIS, G119.

Putnoe
See BEDFORD, G17.

Radwell
See FELMERSHAM, G90.

RAVENSDEN (Map B)

204. Pottery, 2nd to 4th century, located by field-walking.
TL 0756.
Inf. Bedford Archaeological Society, 1979.
SMR 1827.

RIDGMONT (Map C)

205. Approximately 200 Roman sherds, with iron and lead fragments, were found by J.B. Graham when Brogborough Hill road diversion was constructed in 1968.
SP 9638.
Inf. Bedford Mus.
SMR 2793.

ROXTON (Map B)

206. A group of rectangular enclosures at Wyboston was examined by C.F. Tebbutt before gravel extraction in the 1950s. It proved to be a farmstead established in the Belgic period, continuing in use in Roman times, though the excavator assumed a gap between the Belgic and Roman occupations on the basis of a silt deposit in the ditches. One interesting feature of the site was the presence of coal in the Roman levels, apparently deriving from Northumberland or Durham, which probably demonstrates communication with North Sea routes via the Fens. (See page 25 and fig. 11).
TL 1757.
CUCAP; C.F. Tebbutt, "A Belgic and Roman Farm at Wyboston, Bedfordshire", *Proceedings of the Cambridge Antiquarian Society* 50, 1957, 75-84.
SMR 476.

207. Examination of a group of Bronze Age ring ditches by A. Taylor and P.J. Woodward in 1972-74, before gravel extraction, showed that the site of the ring-ditches was being ploughed by the Roman period. Field boundary ditches were laid out probably at the end of the 1st century AD. Evidence of a 2nd or 3rd century habitation site included pits and the post-holes of timber buildings. Fragments of pipeclay figurines suggest the existence of a religious site in the vicinity. (See pages 41 and 56).
TL 1553.
Brit. 5, 1974, 435; Taylor and Woodward, 1982 forthcoming.
SMR 617.

208. Pottery found in 1960.
TL 1757.
OS (C.F. Tebbutt).
SMR 479.

209. A Roman jar containing cremated bones was found in Palace Yard Wood in the late 1960s.
TL 1354.
Inf. Bedford Mus.
SMR 5052.

Ruxox
See MAULDEN, G174.

Salford
See HULCOTE and SALFORD.

SANDY (Map E)

There have been large numbers of references to Roman finds from Sandy, beginning in the 17th century with John Aubrey's much-quoted description of an urn "red, like coral" (a samian vessel) from Chesterfield (see Johnston, 1974, 37). Early antiquaries took the name Salinae from the Ptolemy's *Geography* and applied it to Sandy on dubious etymological grounds, e.g. R. Blome (*Britannia*, 1673, 45, quoted in Watkin, 1882, 269): "Also at *Sande* and *Chesterfield*, near adjoyning, which is now nothing but a warren, stood the famous city of *Salena* of the Romans, which by the ruins of its walls (in many places yet to be seen) doth declare it to have been a place of large extent." This reference to walls probably results from a confusion with the earthworks of the Iron Age hillfort, Caesar's Camp (which itself is inappropriately named), and the impression it gives of a Roman walled town has perhaps tended to give Sandy the appearance of a higher status than the other evidence merits. The most complete summary is that by Johnston (1974), where all previous references are listed and discussed, and many of the finds published. (See pages 7-8, 28 and 30-1).

The main settlement

210. The first area at Sandy to produce substantial evidence of the Roman occupation was the significantly named Chesterfield. This land has been devoted for several centuries to market gardening, which is labour intensive, close work, and this explains the large number of coins and small artefacts which have been reported (see page 31), including a mirror, a bronze female head (see page 45), and an intaglio ring, with an apparently Christian emblem (see page 60). A bronze plaque showing the head of Mercury was found in 1890 (see page 56 and fig. 58). Glass and pottery vessels containing ashes suggest cremation burials, which D.E. Johnston has interpreted as roadside burials south of the main settlement. Brick, tile and sandstone scattered on the field's surface indicate the presence of buildings (see page 52).

The field lies across the line of the Roman road from Baldock; its surface has been encountered during ploughing and dug out for its metalling in recent times (see pages 64-5).

TL 1848.
Johnston, 1974, esp. pp. 35-37.
SMR 444.

211. From *c*.1850, emphasis shifted to the line of the Great Northern Railway, then under construction, and to a gravel pit at Tower Hill to the west, which provided ballast for the track. The main finds were cremation urns and inhumation burials, indicating that the small gravel knoll had served as a cemetery for the settlement to the east. The occurrence of both cremation and inhumation burials suggests a long life for the cemetery, with cremation in the earlier period being replaced by inhumation in the later. Two of the inhumations were in lead coffins and one was found with a pewter bowl.

A deposit of "nearly 30 quarters" of charred wheat, was perhaps a batch of grain being dried or malted in the drying kiln. (See pages 7-8, 31, 34, 41-2, 47 and 60-1, and figs. 1, 28 and 34b).

TL 1748.

Johnston, 1974, esp. pp. 40-41; Taddy, 1853.

SMR 11318.

212. Many of the finds from Sandy in recent decades have derived from the municipal cemetery, situated in the north corner of Chesterfield. There is some evidence of building remains, in layers of "crumbled brick" and a surface of flat sandstone. Refuse pits produced large quantities of broken pottery, a fragment of glass vessel (fig. 50), a pewter dish and bronze ornaments. One pit contained three skeletons, buried head first. A hard metalled surface running east-north-east/west-south-west (at right angles to the Godmanchester road) may have been one of the main streets of the settlement. Many of the finds and pottery from the cemetery date from the 1st and 2nd centuries. (See pages 31, 35-6, 51 and 72, and fig. 29d).

TL 1748-1848.
Johnston, 1974, esp. pp. 38-39.
SMR 11313.

213. In 1954, D.E. Johnston conducted some small excavations near 'The Bungalow' in Stratford Road. A ditch associated with Belgic occupation had been back-filled in early Roman times, and the top consolidated with a layer of rammed gravel, which was interpreted as being the main Baldock-Sandy Roman road. Roman pottery nearby showed that occupation continued in the area.

TL 1848.
Johnston, 1974, esp. pp. 37-38.
SMR 11311.

214. Construction of a house extension in Stratford Road in 1979 revealed a pit containing Belgic pottery, while unstratified sherds and a bronze pin demonstrated occupation in the Roman period.

TL 1848.
Inf. author.
SMR 11323.

215. A number of finds were reported to have come from the branch railway between Sandy and Potton. This line was linked into the main line as it passed through Sandy, so these discoveries may well have come from the same general area as the rest of the 19th century finds. The most notable is a group of three bronze bowls, thought by Kennett to be of late Roman date, which was probably deposited as a hoard. A fourth bowl from Sandy was purchased by the British Museum in 1900. (See pages 46, 49 and 59, and fig. 39).

c.TL 1847-1848.

David H. Kennett, "Late Roman Bronze Vessel Hoards in Britain", *Jahrbuch des Römisch-Germanischen Zentralmuseums Mainz* 16, 1969, 123-148; David H. Kennett, "A Roman Bronze Bowl from Sandy", *Beds. Arch. J.* 6, 1971, 74.

SMR 11319.

216. During gravel quarrying in 1981, a spread of Roman finds was identified lying immediately over gravel at a depth of 1.5 metres (5 feet). The overlying deposits had been marsh at some time, and the finds probably represent disposal of rubbish from the main settlement. Many coins were collected, but remained in private hands. A 4th century pewter bowl had been found in the area some months previously. (See page 31).

TL 1748.

Inf. author; Stephen Greep, "A Late Roman Pewter Vessel from Sandy", *Beds. Arch. J.* 18, 1984 forthcoming.

SMR 548.

217. Many other finds have been reported which probably came from the area of the main settlement at Sandy, but for which the findspots were not recorded or are uncertain. These largely consist of coins and pottery, but also include some brooches, a lead ingot (see page 47), the lower part of a rotary quern (fig. 20a), a bronze handle with Medusa head (fig. 59) and the iron coulter from a plough (see page 48 and fig. 44). A hoard of ironwork was found in the late 19th century; it comprises mainly cart-fittings, but also other objects, such as a farrier's buttress, a mower's anvil and a cobbler's last (see pages 35, 48, 48n57 and 59). W.H. Manning concluded that while few of the objects are closely datable, the group as a whole would not be out of place in the 4th century. In analysing the coins R. Reece believes there may have been a Theodosian hoard of AD 400 which has strayed into the list of general finds; this confirms the general air of unrest at the end of the 4th century (see page 72). Some off-cuts of bronze may indicate the manufacture of bronze objects (see page 43).

*c.*TL 1748-1848.

Johnston, 1974, *passim*; Manning, 1964; W.H. Manning, "Ironwork Hoards in Iron Age and Roman Britian", *Brit.* 3, 1972, 224-250, esp. p. 235.

SMR 11324.

218. An oculist's stamp was found in 1873, probably in the Tower Hill cemetery. The inscriptions read: (1) C VAL AMANDI/DIOXVM AD REVMATIC(um); (2) C VAL VALENTINI/ DIAGLAVC(ium) POST IMP(etum) LIP(pitudinis); (3) C VAL AMANDI/STACTUM AD CAL(iginem); (4) C VAL VALENTINI/ MIXTVM AD CL(aritudinem). They can be translated: (1) Gaius Valerius Amandus' vinegar salve for running eyes; (2) Gaius Valerius Valentinus' celandine ointment to be used after an attack of inflammation of the eyes; (3) Gaius Valerius Amandus' drops for poor sight; (4) Gaius Valerius Valentinus' mixture for clearing the eyes. (See page 54).

*c.*TL 1748.

Johnston, 1974, 46-47.

SMR 462.

Other sites

219. At Furzenhall Farm, a square enclosure, photographed from the air, was still visible as a slight bank on the ground in the 1950s. Excavations by D.E. Johnston in 1959 produced 3rd to 4th century pottery and slight evidence of buildings, with some traces of earlier occupation.

TL 1947.

CUCAP; Johnston, 1974, 51.

SMR 446.

220 A coin of Magnus Maximus (AD 383-388) and a bronze toilet implement, found during house-building, were brought in to Bedford Museum for identification in 1975. In 1981, some pottery of 2nd century date was discovered, along with some human bones. The site lies on gravels, approximately one mile (1.6 km) north-west of the main Roman complex at Sandy, and probably represents a river valley farmstead.

TL 1649-1650.

Inf. Bedford Mus; Brian Dix and Pat Aird, "Second Century A.D. Pottery from Sandy, Bedfordshire", *Beds. Arch. J.* 16, 1982 forthcoming.

SMR 6612.

221. Roman pottery has been found at All Saints' Church, London Road.

TL 1649.

Johnston, 1974, 39.

SMR 11310.

SHARNBROOK (Map A)

222. Early Roman pottery, located by field-walking.

SP 9959.

Hall and Hutchings, 1972, 10.

SMR 2684.

SHEFFORD (Map D)

223. Thomas Inskip, a local antiquary, kept a close watch on gravel pits in the Shefford area in the early 19th century, and identified a wealthy Roman cemetery to the west of the town in 1826. Among the cremation burials he recovered large quantities of samian and other pottery, an amphora, glass and bronze vessels, coins from Vespasian (AD 69-79) to Constantius II (AD 324-361), and various other objects, including those described as an iron lamp, a silver pipe and a lead eagle. He reported that the rectangular burial ground was surrounded by a wall of sandstone. Believing there would be a temple in the vicinity, he searched for it about ten years later, and located a rectangular building (which he assumed to be the temple), associated with which he described "a trench or cist, about twelve feet (3.5 metres) long, filled with ashes, burnt bone and charcoal. Over this were Roman tiles leaning against each other . ."; this sounds very like a hypocaust channel.

D.H. Kennett has examined the surviving glass and bronze vessels and concludes that they are of 1st century date, while a Terra Nigra platter in the pottery collection would not have been imported from the continent much later than the mid-1st century AD, though of course may have been buried at a later date. Unfortunately the samian from the site was confused with that from the Stanfordbury burials (G231), and cannot be used to give precise dating evidence.

In 1940, Mr Gray rapidly re-examined the "temple" site before the area was levelled for a school playing field, and demonstrated that it was indeed a Roman domestic building with a hypocaust. (See pages 8, 18, 27-8, 51 and 60, and fig. 48).

> TL 1338.
> Dryden, 1845, 8-15; Thomas Inskip, *Arch. J.* 1, 1846, 395-398; Inskip, 1850, 166; Fox, 1923, 201-205; inf. Bedford Mus.
> SMR 379.

SHILLINGTON (Map G)

224. Scatters of pottery and stone, located by field-walking.

> TL 1231.
> Inf. R. White, 1978.
> SMR 9298.

225. Two quernstones were found in the 1950s when a field was turned from pasture to arable, and some samian pottery was collected from the surface in 1978. Enclosure cropmarks have also been recorded.

> TL 1231.
> CUCAP; inf. R.F. White, 1978.
> SMR 1841.

226. A burial with a Nene valley colour-coated beaker was found during chalk quarrying.

> TL 1331.
> Inf. R. White, 1978; Cambridge Mus.
> SMR 3044.

227. On Pegsdon Common, on the spring line at the foot of the chalk downs, W. Ransom excavated some cremations in 1879.

> TL 1230.
> Ransom, 1886, 39; *VCH Herts.* 4, 1914, 159.
> SMR 413.

228. In 1932, the excavation of a dew pond close to the Icknield Way revealed a ditch with 2nd or 3rd century pottery and a coin of Antoninus Pius (AD 138-160).

> TL 1129.
> Ralph J. Whiteman (ed.), *Hexton: A Parish Survey*, 1936, 181-182.
> SMR 9291.

229. A penannular bronze brooch, from Apsley End. (See fig. 34d).

> c.TL 1232.
> Inf. Luton Mus.
> SMR 1986.

SILSOE (Map D)

230. A pottery vessel from Silsoe in Thomas Inskip's collection contains cremated bones.

> Unprov.
> Inf. Cambridge Mus.
> SMR 12146.

SOUTHILL (Map D)

231. At Stanfordbury, two very wealthy Belgic cremation burials were uncovered in the early 1830s. The first was located during drainage works and further finds were made by Thomas Inskip. He described two "vaults". The first contained amphorae, samian and bronze vessels, iron fire-dogs, spits and a tripod, a bone "flute" (probably a cylindrical hinge) and black and white "gaming pieces". The second also contained amphorae, samian and glass vessels, with personal ornaments (beads, brooches, a shale bracelet) and the bronze fittings from a box. The floors of the burial places were reported to be paved with Roman tiles. While some of the finds have been lost, and the samian vessels

mixed with those from Shefford (G223), the surviving evidence suggests a mid-1st century date for the burials, probably immediately after the Roman invasion. (See pages 8, 15, 18, 28, 41, 51 and 60).

TL 1441.

Dryden, 1845, 15-20; Inskip, 1850, 166-169; Reginald A. Smith, *Arch*. 63, 1911, 9-12; Fox, 1923, 99-100, 105, 189-190 & 202-205; I.M. Stead, "A La Tene III Burial at Welwyn Garden City", *Arch*. 101, 1967, 1-62, esp. pp.47 & 55-56; Peacock, 1971, 165 & 182.

SMR 457.

STANBRIDGE (Map F)

232. On Harlington Hill, just above a spring called Bretch'll, F.G. Gurney collected Roman pottery. There is also some tile, plaster and mortar from Gurney's collection from the site in Luton Museum.

SP 9524.

CRO: X325/66 & 110, Gurney notebooks 1917-22; inf. Luton Mus.

SMR 1434.

233. A hilltop scatter of Roman material, above a spring known as Stockwell. (See page 74).

SP 9624.

CRO: X325/66 & 145, Gurney notebook, 1922.

SMR 3220.

234. Pottery.

SP 9423.

F.G. Gurney map in Luton Mus., acc. no. 5/50/60.

SMR 12748.

Stanfordbury

See SOUTHILL, G231.

STAPLOE (Map B)

235. Pits and ditches containing Roman pottery were excavated in 1935.

TL 1461.

OS (C.F. Tebbutt, 1949).

SMR 496.

STOTFOLD (Map E)

236. Post-holes were recorded by D.C. King during building development in 1969, and a number of finds collected, including Belgic pottery, samian and colour-coated ware, nails, brooches and a quern.

TL 2236.

Beds. Arch. J. 5, 1970, 124.

SMR 74.

237. Pottery and bones found during building on Bury Farm, *c*.1964.

TL 2236.

Inf. Luton Mus.

SMR 11327.

238. Belgic and Roman pottery, found in the "Two Chimneys" sandpit.

TL 2033.

OS (J. Morris, 1958).

SMR 508.

STREATLEY (Map G)

239. Roman pottery was found on Sharpenhoe Clappers during excavations by Brian Dix in 1979. No Roman features were identified though there was probably occupation in the vicinity.

TL 0630.

Brian Dix, "An Excavation at Sharpenhoe Clappers, Streatley, Bedfordshire", *Beds. Arch. J.* 16, 1982 forthcoming.

SMR 238.

240. On Galley Hill, overlooking the Icknield Way, one of a pair of barrows was excavated by James Dyer in 1951 and 1961. A number of skeletons had been added to the surface of the barrow, of which twelve were attributed to a slaughter cemetery of the 4th century, on the basis of associated coins. The rest were thought to be burials from the late medieval gallows on the site. While there is no reason to doubt the late Roman date given for the group of twelve, there seems no clear evidence to justify describing it as a slaughter cemetery. It is more likely to have been the burial place for a small settlement somewhere on the hilltop. (See page 72).

TL 0926.

James Dyer, "The Excavation of Two Barrows on Galley Hill, Streatley", *Beds. Arch. J.* 9, 1974, 13-34.

SMR 116.

SUNDON (Map G)

241. A few sherds of pottery with burnt pebbles, located by field-walking.

TL 0528.

Inf. D. Hall, 1978.

SMR 9341.

242. A dark area of soil with Roman sherds, located by field-walking.

TL 0628.

Inf. D. Hall, 1978.

SMR 9334.

243. Occupation, with pottery and stone, located by field-walking.

 TL 0427.
 Inf. D. Hall, 1978.
 SMR 9309.

244. Large Iron Age settlement with some Belgic and Roman material, located by field-walking.

 TL 0527.
 Inf. D. Hall, 1978.
 SMR 9310.

245. Occupation, with a large quantity of sherds and some quernstones; located by field-walking.

 TL 0627.
 Inf. D. Hall, 1978.
 SMR 9333.

TEMPSFORD (Map B)

246. An occupation site was identified after deep ploughing during the winter of 1961-2, producing high quality pottery, metal objects, roof tiles and building materials. A small excavation was carried out by G.T. Rudd, who interpreted the features located as part of the industrial area of Roman villa, on the basis of pits filled with ash and pottery wasters. Ashlar blocks, tesserae and marble wall-facings indicated a luxurious building in the vicinity, but it was not located. Among the finds was a large number of 3rd century coins. (See pages 27, 41, 48-9 and 52, and figs. 24a & b, 46b, and 47b & c).

 TL 1652.
 Granville T. Rudd, "The trial excavation of a Roman Site at Tempsford in 1962", *Beds. Arch. J.* 2, 1964, 78.
 SMR 801.

247. Roman occupation was revealed when sewage works were built in the vicinity of a cropmark site, composed of a group of rectilinear enclosures with associated trackway. A pit with Roman pottery, and post-holes of early Roman date, were noted by C.F. Tebbutt.

 TL 1654.
 CUCAP; OS, (Tebbutt, undated).
 SMR 1671.

THURLEIGH (Map A)

248. Occupation with 4th century colour-coated pottery and undressed stone, located by field-walking.

 TL 0458.
 Hall and Hutchings, 1972, 11; OS, 1977.
 SMR 2709.

249. Excavations by E. Baker and the author on the outer earthworks of Thurleigh medieval castle in 1976 revealed early Roman occupation in the form of ditches and pits.

 TL 0558.
 CBA Gp. 9 NL 7, 1977, 20-22; *Brit.* 8, 1977, 400.
 SMR 313.

250. Iron slag with pottery, located by field-walking.

 TL 0556.
 Hall and Hutchings, 1972, 11.
 SMR 2729.

251. Wide scatter of pottery, located by field-walking.

 TL 0556.
 Hall and Hutchings, 1972, 11.
 SMR 2736.

252. Slag patch with Iron Age and Roman pottery, located by field-walking.

 TL 0456.
 Hall and Hutchings, 1972, 11.
 SMR 2715.

253. Slag patch with Iron Age and Roman pottery, located by field-walking.

 TL 0556.
 Hall and Hutchings, 1972, 11.
 SMR 2713.

254. Pottery scatter, located by field-walking.

 TL 0556.
 Hall and Hutchings, 1972, 11.
 SMR 2722.

TILSWORTH (Map F)

255. A spread of pottery and tile, located by field-walking, 1974.

 SP 9825.
 Inf. J. Schneider.
 SMR 1763.

256. Several sherds of pottery, located by field-walking.

 SP 9724.
 Inf. J. Schneider, 1972.
 SMR 2804.

TINGRITH (Map F)

257. A hoard of more than 2000 coins in a pottery vessel was found during sand extraction in 1961. A high proportion of the coins were in mint condition, and the burial date was probably between AD 335 and AD 337. An area of burnt soil with the remains of a cooking pot was found about 3 feet (1 metre) from the

hoard. (See page 72).

TL 0133.

JRS 53, 1963, 136; T.H. Gardner, "Some General Observations on the Tingrith Hoard", *Manshead Mag.* 13, Oct. 1964, 28-30.

SMR 236.

TODDINGTON (Map F)

258. On Sheepwalk Hill, Anglo-Saxon skeletons were found in the 19th century. One of the burials was found "lying on a bed of concrete four to six inches thick, and not less than nine feet square" (100 to 150 mm by 2.75 metres square). It was reported to be "made of lime and pebbles, and was sufficiently hard to resist the shovel". This sounds very like the floor of a substantial Roman building. (See pages 27 and 52).

TL 0229.

Maj. W. Cooper Cooper, *PSA* (2nd series) 10, 1883-5, 37; *VCH Beds.* 1, 1904, 185.

SMR 101.

259. On a knoll called Foxburrow, drainage works in 1874 revealed Roman finds. Major W. Cooper Cooper and J. Wyatt investigated the site and reported the discovery of large quantities of pottery fragments, animal bones, and charred wood and stones. Major Cooper interpreted it as a burial place, but clay kiln bars in Luton Museum show it to have been a pottery manufacturing site. The field known as Foxburrow is now occupied by the Toddington service station of the M1 motorway. (See page 40).

TL 0228-0328.

James Wyatt, *PSA* (2nd series) 6, 1873-6, 184-187; Maj. W. Cooper Cooper, *PSA* (2nd series) 10, 1883-5, 133-134; Page and Keate, 1908, 14-15; inf. Luton Museum.

SMR 95.

260. From claypits at Fancott, Roman pottery was found during the 19th century. Lumps of copper and wood charcoal may indicate associated bronze-working activity. (See page 43).

TL 0127-0227.

CRO: X325/53, F.G. Gurney notebook, 1913-14; Blundell, 1925, 3.

SMR 90.

261. A spread of Roman pottery was discovered to the south-west of Chalton by the Manshead Archaeological Society in 1962. The Society photographed it from the air and reported a number of square fields and the outlines of a small building. Trial excavations produced 3rd and 4th century pottery, animal bones and iron objects, but no evidence of buildings. Brick,

roof tile and flint cobbles have since been identified by field-walking, with Roman material spread over an area approximately 600 metres (2000 feet) square.

TL 0226.

Manshead Mag. 9, Aug. 1962, 143-144; 10, Dec. 1962, 12; OS, 1973.

SMR 1438.

262. Roman pottery was discovered at Chalton when the Midland Railway was constructed in 1865. When the railway was being widened in the 1890s, a 40 feet (12 metres) deep Roman well was revealed, containing pottery and animal bones.

TL 0426.

F.W. Crick, "Discovery of an Old Roman Well", *BNQ* 3, 1893, 63-64; inf. Luton Museum.

SMR 6659.

263. A small bronze elephant, thought to be Roman, was found while digging a ditch on Lodge Farm in 1836.

TL 0031.

John Bowyer Nichols, *Arch.* 28, 1840, 434; Blundell, 1925, 4.

SMR 1412.

264. Several coins found near Toddington Church.

TL 0028-0128.

Inf. Luton Mus.

SMR 6573.

See also CHALGRAVE, G53.

TOTTERNHOE (Map F)

265. A courtyard villa at Totternhoe was identified and partly excavated by the Manshead Archaeological Society in 1954. It had a bath block, mosaic and tessellated pavements, and painted wall-plaster. The walls were of flint and sandstone. The villa has been given a 4th century date, and there is evidence of decay towards the end of its life. A quantity of 2nd century pottery suggests an earlier building on or near the same site. A sherd of 5th century Saxon pottery indicates that the site was occupied to some extent in the early post-Roman period. (See pages 25-6, 29, 38, 52-3 and 74, and figs. 12-13).

SP 9820.

JRS 47, 1957, 214; Matthews, 1963, 61-65; OS, 1954.

SMR 534.

266. Shirrell Spring is reported to have produced "hundreds of Romano-British potsherds", as well as Roman coins and pins, which may indicate a sacred site or adjacent settlement. (See page 56).

SP 9822.

Gurney, 1920, 168n10; F.G. Gurney map in Luton Mus., acc. no. 7/50/60.

SMR 26.

267. F.G. Gurney collected Roman potsherds in an area of chalk quarrying in 1922.

SP 9822.

CRO: X325/66, Gurney notebook, 1922.

SMR 24.

268. A spread of 3rd to 4th century sherds below ploughsoil was revealed during chalk quarrying in 1971.

SP 9822.

Matthews, 1962, 131; inf. Manshead Arch. Soc.

SMR 1957.

269. Pits containing Roman pottery, tiles and animal bones were found in 1899.

SP 9821.

Smith, 1904, 52 & 54.

SMR 25.

270. Rev S.A. Woolward excavated a "Roman-British hut" in 1895, from which he collected a broken quern of Andernach lava, a knife, a Roman tile with a dog's paw print, and flint flakes. Nearby were two fragmentary human skulls. F.G. Gurney also found Roman pottery in the area. (See page 34n4).

SP 9820.

Smith, 1904, 57; CRO: X325/149, Gurney notebook, 1913-14.

SMR 140.

271. When the Anglo-Saxon cemetery at Marina Drive, Dunstable (in Totternhoe parish) was being excavated by the Manshead Archaeological Society, many worn Roman sherds were found in the fill of the Saxon graves. A ditch was identified, containing a late Roman sherd, and it is probable that the area was farmed in the Roman period from a nearby settlement.

TL 0021.

C.L. Matthews, "The Anglo-Saxon Cemetery at Marina Drive, Dunstable", *Beds. Arch. J.* 1, 1962, 25-47.

SMR 152.

272. In 1769 or 1770, a labourer digging for "gravel" (probably meaning flints for road surfacing) found a coin hoard in a pottery jar. The coins were reported to be of Antoninus and Constantine. (See pages 8 and 75).

TL 0019.

Brandreth, 1838, 104; Smith, 1904, 184.

SMR 104.

273. A bronze winged phallus (a popular classical good luck emblem), with a ring for suspension as an ornament. (See page 59).

Unprov.

Smith, 1904, 53; W.G. Smith, *PSA* (2nd series) 21, 1906-7, 82.

SMR 7090.

TURVEY (Map A)

274. An area of Roman occupation has produced pottery (including samian and colour-coated ware), roof tiles, a possible kiln bar, iron slag, and a lead object which may have been used as a weight.

SP 9551.

BNFAS 4, Apr. 1970, 13; *Beds. Arch. J.* 6, 1971, 88; OS, 1973.

SMR 1186.

275. Coins of Trajan (AD 97-117) and Hadrian (AD 117-138) were found "at Baden" in 1858. Nearby cropmarks of rectilinear enclosures and trackways in a field known as "Stony Hill" in 1902 (CRO: HG 116) may be a Roman settlement from which these coins came.

SP 9553.

Gent's Mag. n.s. 6, 1859, 397; NMR AP.

SMR 1418 and 2431.

276. A coarse pot, containing "some small copper money", was found while digging some ground for tree-planting in 1826. A coin of Constantine (AD 306-337) was found nearby.

SP 9451.

CRO: Longuet-Higgins scrap-book (mic. 84), p. 12.

SMR 3376.

WHIPSNADE (Map F)

277. Excavation of clay for brick kilns at Kensworth Common in the late 19th and early 20th centuries uncovered a great quantity of Roman material, recorded and in part collected by W.G. Smith. Some complete vessels indicate cremation burials, but broken pottery, querns, tiles, loomweights (see fig. 22) and animal bones, and a reference to "waste pits . . . found in large numbers", suggest there was an associated settlement, though no structures were recorded.

The clay pits from which the finds were recovered actually lie within Whipsnade, not Kensworth, parish (see Alan Cox, *Brickmaking: A*

History and Gazetteer, Bedfordshire County Council and Royal Commission on Historical Monuments, 1979, 103-104).

> TL 0317.
> Smith, 1904, 52-54, 134-135.
> SMR 107.

WILLINGTON (Map D)

278. The most complex and extensive cropmark site of the Roman period in the county lies in the parishes of Willington and Cople. A series of enclosures covers nearly two square kilometres (0.75 square mile), and shows several phases of re-arrangement of field boundaries. Regular cropmarks at one end of the complex may relate to a villa site. Roman pottery has been reported from the area. (See pages 32 and 65-6, and figs. 18, 63 and 64).

> TL 1148.
> CUCAP; NMR AP; David E. Johnston, *Beds. Times*, 21 Mar. 1958, p. 12.
> SMR 1861.

279. Cropmarks have been photographed in an area where Roman material was discovered in 1860. A skeleton, querns and a quantity of pottery (including samian) were found during drainage works, with a coin of Magnentius (AD 350-353).

> TL 1249.
> Watkin, 1882, 282; *BAAS Notes*, vol. 1, no. 9, Jun. 1861, 143-144; CUCAP.
> SMR 1860.

280. Early Roman occupation was discovered during excavations in advance of gravel extraction, in December 1983.

> TL 1050.
> Inf. A. Pinder.
> SMR 1478.

WILSTEAD (Map D)

281. An area of cropmarks has produced surface finds of the Roman period. D.C. King has collected a large quantity of pottery, two coins of Severus (AD 193-211), and two of Gallienus (AD 253-268), roof and floor tiles, nails, quern fragments, and bronze and iron objects, showing occupation from the Belgic period to the late 4th century.

> TL 0745.
> CUCAP; *Beds. Arch. J.* 6, 1971, 85; inf. D.C. King, 1973.
> SMR 1181.

282. A report of kiln bars and wasters suggests a pottery kiln site.

> TL 0744.
> Inf. D.C. King, 1973.
> SMR 3637.

WOBURN (Map C)

283. Amphorae from Woburn Park suggest a Belgic or early Roman cremation burial.

> Unprov.
> Duke of Bedford, "Roman Amphora found in the Park at Woburn Abbey", *Arch.* 25, 1834, 606-607; Page and Keate, 1908, 15; Peacock, 1971, 182.
> SMR 38.

Wyboston

> See ROXTON, G206.

WYMINGTON (Map A)

284. A surface scatter of occupation debris, including stone, brick, a quern and 3rd century pottery; located by field-walking.

> SP 9464.
> Inf. J. Moore, 1978.
> SMR 1916.

285. Occupation site, producing pottery (including colour-coated ware) and a quern fragment, located by field-walking.

> SP 9564.
> Hall and Hutchings, 1972, 12.
> SMR 2756.

286. Occupation, covering about two acres, with some building material and a quern fragment, located by field-walking.

> SP 9664.
> Hall and Hutchings, 1972, 12.
> SMR 2757.

287. A small area of pottery with stone and pebbles, located by field-walking.

> SP 9663.
> Hall and Hutchings, 1972, 12.
> SMR 2758.

288. A Belgic and Roman occupation site covering about one acre, with pottery (including colour-coated ware), stone and roof tiles; located by field-walking.

> SP 9563.
> Hall and Hutchings, 1972, 12.
> SMR 2759.

Yielden

> See MELCHBOURNE and YIELDEN.

INDEX

Where individual sites are discussed in the text, the relevant page numbers can also be found in the gazetteer entries.

G119, map F

Putnoe (Bedford), *figs. 25, 43*, G17, map D

quarries, 52, 61

querns, 34, *fig. 20*, G22, G39, G42, G46, G64, G120, G132, G185, G202, G217, G225, G236, G245, G270, G277, G279, G281, G284-6

Radwell (Felmersham), 27, 38n16, 48, 51, G90, map A

rake, 48

Ravensden, G204, map B

religion, 55-62

    head cult, 55, 57-8, 62

    imperial cult, 55

    water cult, 55, 57-8

religious sites, 8, 27, 32, 55, 60, G53, G174, G207, G266

Ridgmont, G205, map C

rings, 42, 44, 61, *figs. 33, 35*, G27, G63, *see also* intaglios

river gravels, 14, 20-1

roads, 63-9, 78-9

    local, 64-6, 78, *figs. 18, 63-6*, G8, G64, G154, G212

    major, 16, 18, 30, 63, 66, 69, 78, *fig. 62, 66*, G210, G213

    pre-Roman, 66, 68-9, *fig. 66*

roof tiles, *see* tiles

Roxton, 41, 55, G206-9, map B, *see also* Wyboston

Ruxox, 28, 31, 35, 48, 55, 59, 74, 78, *figs. 7-8, 24, 35, 47, 54-5*, G174, map D

Scheduled Ancient Monuments, 77

Salford, *see* Hulcote and Salford

Salinae, 30-1, G(Sandy)

sandstone, 52, G150, G210, G212, G223, G265

Sandy, 7-8, 18, 24, 28, 30-1, 36, 38, 41-2, 45-8, 48n57, 50-2, 54-5, 59-61, 64-6, 72-4, 77-8, *figs. 1, 5-8, 20, 28-30, 34, 39, 44, 50, 58-9, 67*, G210-21, map E, *see also* Chesterfield, Galley Hill

Saxon, *see* Anglo-Saxon

scallops, 38

Scots, 70

sculpture, 28, 55, *fig. 56*, G23

seal box, 45, *fig. 37*

Severn, R., 16

shale, 15, 51, 61, G191, G231

Sharnbrook, G222, map A

Sharpenhoe (Streatley), 78, G239, map G

sheep, 34-5

Shefford, 8, 18, 27-8, 51, 60, *fig. 48*, G223, map D

shellfish, 38, *see also* oysters, scallops, whelks

Shillington, *fig. 34*, G224-G229, map G, *see also* Pegsdon

Shirrell Spring (Totternhoe), 55, G266, map F

shrines, *see* religious sites

sickle, 48

Silchester, *fig. 6*

Silsoe, G230, map D

silver, 42, G223

small towns, *see* towns

Smith, Worthington G., 9

social hierarchy, 11, 14, 18, 21, 24-5, 28-31, 33

Southill, G231, map D, *see also* Stanfordbury

spatula, 44, *see also* ligula

spearhead, 49, *fig. 47*

spindlewhorls, 35, 39, *fig. 21*

spits, 15, G231

St Albans, *see* Verulamium

Stanbridge, 10, 74, G232-4, map F

Stanfordbury (Southill) 8, 15, 18, 28, 51, 60, *fig. 5*, G231, map D

Staploe, G235, map B

stone, *see* clunch, flint, limestone, sandstone

steelyards, 45-6, *fig. 38*, G38, G210

Stotfold, G236-8, map E

Streatley, 78, G239-40, map G, *see also* Galley Hill, Sharpenhoe

stylus, 45, *fig. 37*

Suetonius Paulinus, 19

Sulis Minerva, 55

Sundon, G241-5, map G

Sussex, 16

swords, 49

Tasciovanus, 12

temples, *see* religious sites

Tempsford, 41, 48-9, 52, *figs. 24, 46-7*, G246-7, map B

tesserae, 27, 54, G32, G127, G174, G177, G246, *see also* mosaics

textiles, 35

Thames, R., 63, *fig. 6*

Theodosius, 70

Thiodweg, 68, *fig. 66*

Thurleigh, G248-54, map A

tile manufacture, 53, G104

tiles

    flue tiles, 27, 52-3, *fig. 52*, G24, G47, G63, G90, G155, G186

    roof riles, 27, 52-3, *fig. 51*, G47, G87, G90, G132, G146, G186, G188, G196, G246, G261, G274, G281, G288

Tilsworth, 74, G255-6, map F

tin, 42, 47

Tingrith, 72, G257, map F

Toddington, 9, 27, 40, 52, 55, G258-64, map F,